Jane

from the

Blanch   Oct 91

THE
SPORTING
COOKBOOK

The SPORTING COOKBOOK

ANGELA F. RAWSON & NIKKI ROWAN-KEDGE

Foreword by LUDOVIC KENNEDY

· THE ·
SPORTSMAN'S
PRESS
LONDON

Published by The Sportsman's Press 1989

British Library Cataloguing in Publication Data
Rawson, Angela F.
The sporting cookbook.
1. Food. Recipes
I. Title   II. Kedge, Nikki R.
641.5

ISBN 0-948253-35-5

Filmset and printed in Great Britain by
BAS Printers Limited, Over Wallop, Hampshire

CONTENTS

ACKNOWLEDGEMENTS

Many people and organisations have given us help and encouragement, allowed us to use illustrations, quote recipes or extracts from books and poems, but we would like particularly to thank the following:

Robert Anderson and Century Hutchinson Publishing Group, London (*Heard in the Slips*); Mrs Nancy Barker and Frank and Jan James for the loan of their precious sporting and antiquarian books; Bestseller Publications Ltd, London (Cecil Aldin's *The Romance of the Road*); Simon Blundell, Librarian, Reform Club, London; The Bowes Museum, Barnhard Castle; Cadogan Books Ltd, London; Stuart Chalk, Kingfisher Photography, Marlborough; Sue Coley, Editor; Frost and Reed, London; David Fuller, Managing Director, Arthur Ackermann & Son, London; *The Field*; Jill Gascoine, Archivist, Reform Club, London; Richard Green Galleries, London; Stephen Green, Curator, Marylebone Cricket Club; Mary and Peter Roberts for the loan of their sporting library; Guinness Publishing Ltd, (*Derby 200*); Ann Harrel, London (*Going to the Moors* by Ronald Eden); Sarah McCance, Assistant Curator, Wimbledon Lawn Tennis Museum; MacConnal-Mason Gallery, London; John Murray (Publishers) Ltd, London (John Betjeman's 'Upper Lambourn'); Stanley Paul & Co Ltd, London (*Mrs Cadogan's Cook Book*).

LIST OF COLOUR PLATES

BLACK AND WHITE ILLUSTRATIONS

FOREWORD
by Ludovic Kennedy

With cookery books in recent years tumbling over one another in profusion, it is a joy to be able to welcome a new one with a difference. The literary extracts from such writers on country affairs as Dickens and Surtees, W.H. Davies and the Rev. Francis Kilvert, provide an apposite filling to the various recipes listed so that the book may be read as much for aesthetic enjoyment as for the mouth-watering sensations of imagining the dishes on the tongue. And what a rich gallimaufry of dishes they are, from old favourites (prepared in the *old* way) like Kedgeree and Queen of Puddings to newcomers (at least to me) like Molasses Spiced Beef in Beer and Black Treacle Soufflé. Fortunate the sportsman or sportswoman returning from a day in the coverts or by the river to find one of these delicacies awaiting them at table.

Those like myself who live within hailing distance of the converted chapel in the Wiltshire village of Rockley where Nikki Rowan-Kedge and Angela Rawson prepare their gastronomic creations will have been able to sample them for themselves. With this book those who live further afield will be in a position to enjoy them too.

Ludovic Kennedy
June 24th 1989

INTRODUCTION

The recipes for this book are based upon the freshest available ingredients. All the produce can be bought from most good butchers, game dealers, or supermarkets.

The dishes themselves have been based on traditional English recipes, catering for the healthy, robust appetites of our sporting ancestors; they have been adapted to suit today's tastes and the availability of ingredients.

We recommend reading through the recipes before cooking; this will ensure that you have all the necessary equipment, ingredients, and allow sufficient time for the preparation.

Measurements are in metric, imperial and [US]. Due to the variation in conversions, in some cases they have been rounded up or down according to the nearest equivalent.

The aim of this book is to enhance healthy and tasty cooking, but to be able to blend and put together delicious food, there must be that vital ingredient which is essential, the love, and the sharing of cooking.

Angela F. Rawson
Nikki Rowan-Kedge

SPRING

When April scatters coins of primrose gold
Among the copper leaves in thickets old
And singing skylarks from the meadows rise
To twinkle like black stars in sunny skies;

Then I go forth on such a pleasant day,
One breath outdoors takes all my care away;
It goes like heavy smoke, when flames take hold
Of wood that's green, and fill a grate with gold.

W. H. Davies (1871–1940)

STILTON AND SPRING ONION [SCALLION] SOUP

Sweet are the sounds that mingle
                    from afar,
Heard by calm lakes, as peeps the
                    folding star,
Where the duck dabbles 'mid the
                    rustling sedge,
And feeding pike starts from the
                    water's edge.
An Evening Walk,
William Wordsworth (1770–1850)

This is a very creamy, delicious soup, easy to make and ideal for any time of the year. When we make it for guests, we have been told that it should carry a government warning as it could become addictive!

To serve 4–6

2 onions, peeled and chopped
1 clove garlic, crushed with a little salt
¾ litre/1½ pints [3¾ cups] chicken or
    vegetable stock
125 g/4 oz [½ cup] unsalted butter
125 g/4 oz Stilton cheese, rind removed
2 sticks celery, washed and chopped
2 carrots, peeled and chopped
1 bunch spring onions [scallions], peeled
    and chopped
125 g/4 oz [½ cup] single [light] cream

Melt the butter in a large, heavy-based pan, add the chopped vegetables and crushed garlic, reserving 2 spring onions [scallions] for garnish. Cook until the vegetables are soft, stirring from time to time.

When the vegetables are cooked, pour in the stock and season well. Simmer for ½ hour, then remove from the heat and crumble the cheese into the liquid. Mix well.

Pureé the soup in a blender then pour into a clean saucepan. Stir in the cream and heat, but do not boil.

The remaining spring onions [scallions] can now be added raw, or sautéed in a little oil and scattered over the soup before serving.

MULLIGATAWNY SOUP

. . . when the heavy lazy mist, which hangs over every object, making the gas-lamps look brighter, and dining parlour curtains are closely drawn, kitchen fires blaze brightly up, and savoury steams of hot dinners salute the nostrils of the hungry wayfarer. . .

Sketches by Boz,
Charles Dickens, 1836–7

This spicy soup was brought over to England from India by British officers and diplomats, among others. It is a very nourishing and tasty soup, ideal for flasks when out in the inclement weather or delicious to come home to after a day in the open air. A good meat stock is necessary for a well-flavoured mulligatawny.

To serve 4–6

4 onions, peeled and chopped
1 clove garlic, crushed with a little salt
1 tbsp mango chutney
5 tsp curry paste
1 litre/2 pints [5 cups] good meat stock, made from the bones of a roast joint
60 g/2 oz diced cooked meat, usually lamb but beef can also be used
2 tbsp beef dripping or fat
2 carrots, peeled and chopped
3 sticks celery, washed and chopped
1 tbsp fresh parsley, chopped
2 tsp tomato pureé [paste]
1 tbsp plain [all purpose] flour
salt and black pepper

Melt the dripping in a large pan, add the chopped onion, carrot, celery and crushed garlic. Cook until the vegetables are soft and just turning brown.

Add the flour, stir thoroughly, and cook for a few minutes to cook the flour. Scrape the pan well to get all the goodness and flavour from the cooked ingredients. Pour in the stock and simmer for 1 hour.

Put the chutney into the soup mixture, add the curry paste, diced meat, and tomato pureé. Season well to taste. Stir and cook for a further 15 minutes. Sprinkle in the parsley and serve with hot crusty bread.

POTTED LOBSTER

An Imperial quart and a half of Mr Creed's stoutest draft port with the orthodox proportion of lemon, cloves, sugar and cinnamon, had almost boiled itself to perfection under the skilful superintendence of Mr Jorrocks, on the coffee-room fire, and a table had been handsomely decorated with shrimps, lobsters, broiled bones, fried ham, poached eggs. . . .
Jorrocks's Jaunts and Jollities, R. S. Surtees, 1838

A dish that would have met with Mr Jorrocks's approval. It is best made with good hen lobsters with their spawn; this aids its creamy texture and delicate flavour.

To serve 4–6

½ kg/1 lb cooked lobster meat
3 tsp anchovy csscncc [cxtract]
60 g/2 oz [4 tbsp] unsalted butter, softened
½ tsp ground mace
2 good pinches cayenne pepper
salt and black pepper
2 tsp chopped parsley
2 tsp clotted or double [heavy] cream.

Pound the lobster meat and mix in all the other ingredients. Alternatively, put all the ingredients into a blender and blend until smooth and creamy.

Spoon into one large pot or individual pots and pour over clarified butter. Allow to set in the refrigerator. Serve with hot toast and a fresh salad.

TO MAKE CLARIFIED BUTTER

¼ kg/8 oz [1 cup] unsalted butter produces about 150 g/5 oz [good ½ cup] clarified butter, and can be used either melted or set.

Melt the unsalted butter in a small saucepan and cook over a gentle heat without stirring until the butter starts to foam. Continue cooking until the butter stops foaming, take care not to brown the butter.

Remove the pan from the heat and allow to stand until the milky deposits have sunk to the bottom of the pan. You should be left with a clear yellow liquid.

Pour the liquid through a clean muslin cloth into a bowl. It can be used straightaway or put in a cool place to set.

KEDGEREE

Khichari, or Kedgeree, originally came from India, and consisted of spices, lentils, rice, fresh limes, onions, fish and butter. It was brought to England in the nineteenth century by members of the East India Company, and it graced the sideboards of the country house dining room for breakfast, alongside silver dishes of kidneys, bacon, eggs and ham. Though the first meal of the day is, for some, not the leisurely affair it used to be, it is none the less an excellent dish on which to start the day, especially as it can be made the day before.

It is very versatile, being good for a light lunch or supper dish, and is easily transportable for picnics. By substituting flaked salmon it becomes a delicious first course for a special party.

To serve 4–6, depending on whether used as a first or main course

½ kg/1 lb smoked haddock
180 g/6 oz [1 cup] long grain rice
2 onions, peeled and chopped
120 g/4 oz [½ cup] unsalted butter
125 ml/¼ pint [½ cup] double [heavy] cream
2 large tbsp chopped parsley
grated rind [zest] and juice of 2 limes or lemons
1 tsp cayenne pepper
1 tsp paprika
¼ litre/½ pint [1¼ cups] milk
6 hard boiled eggs, shells removed (2 for decoration)
salt and black pepper

Put the milk into a saucepan, add the haddock and poach until tender. Remove the fish and reserve the milk. Skin and bone the haddock and flake the meat. Put to one side. Melt the butter in a pan and fry the chopped onion until just turning brown. Chop four of the hard boiled eggs and put these into the pan. Add all the remaining ingredients, except the cream and rice. Mix round thoroughly until all the ingredients are well blended.

Cook the rice in the poaching milk, cover with a little water if necessary. Cook the rice until it has absorbed the liquid and is light and fluffy.

Drain off any remaining liquid and add the rice to the rest of the ingredients.

Mix well together. Stir in the double [heavy] cream, and pile the kedgeree into an oven proof dish to keep warm until required.

If the dish is prepared in advance, on the day required, dot with knobs of butter, cover and heat in a moderate oven for abour 45 to 50 minutes.

Serve decorated with the remaining two chopped hard boiled eggs and sprigs of fresh parsley, also lemon wedges if desired.

POTTED SHRIMPS

There was a little house that said 'Shrimp Teas'. We went through a little wicket gate down a flagged yard (for it was in the grey north). There was a holly bush growing over a stone wall and a wooden bench went along the wall. There were three strong round wooden tables and against the three tables leant twelve strong square wooden chairs. On the tables were white cloths. You went to the door and told Betsy 'We've come'. Then you sat down and 'drew in'.

Betsy brought out a pot of tea, with a woollen tea-cosy on it, sugar and cream, a cup and saucer each, two big plates of thin bread and butter – brown and white – a big green plate of watercress, and a big pink plate of shrimps. And that was all, except an armoured salt celler and a robin. Then you 'reached too'.

Presently Betsy came out again, with a big white apron over her black gown, took the tea pot in to replenish it, and see if you wanted any more bread and butter (you always did).

Food in England,
Dorothy Hartley, 1954

This was Betsy Tatterstall's recipe

'Weigh the shrimps, and take an equal quantity of fine flaked fish (white). Shell the shrimps, and put heads and shells to boil in enough water to cover. Drain, remove shells and heads, and now cook the flaked fish in this shrimp water till soft. Let cool, and pound to a smooth paste with a careful seasoning of powdered mace, cayenne and one single spot of anchovy sauce. Now measure an almost equal quantity of butter. When smooth, stir in all the whole shrimps, make all piping hot, press into pots, and flood with melted butter on the top.

The effect was a solid potful of shrimps, cemented together with a soft, delicately seasoned pink butter. It was a great delicacy, and always served in fine white china.'

HOT PEPPERED CHEESE TARTLETS

The piece of flummery being delivered, the bottles and dessert circulated, and in due time, the ladies retired, the Misses to the drawing room, Madam to the pantry, to see that the Bumbler had not pocketed any of the cheesecakes or tarts, for which, boy-like, he had a propensity. . . .

Ask Mama, R. S. Surtees, 1858

These cheese tartlets are ideal for a first course, a savoury, or as a light main course dish. A good-flavoured Cheddar or a smoked cheese gives a strong flavour. We use an Applewood smoked cheese, which is a mature Cheddar, smoked, with an outer coating of paprika.

If using this recipe for a main dish, the quantities will need to be increased.

To make 20–24 small tartlets

For the filling
90 g/3 oz [scant cup] Cheddar cheese or
    Applewood smoked, finely grated
250 g/8 oz carton cottage cheese
1 large or 2 small eggs
cayenne pepper to taste
black pepper
125 ml/¼ pint [½ cup] single [light] cream
1 tsp salt
For the pastry
90 g/3 oz [6 tbsp] butter
90 g/3 oz [scant cup] Cheddar cheese,
    finely grated
pinch of salt
125 g/4 oz [1 cup] plain [all purpose] flour
¼ tsp cayenne pepper

To make the pastry, cream the butter and cheese together until soft. Gradually work in the flour, cayenne pepper and salt using a wooden spoon. Alternatively, put all the ingredients into a food blender and blend until the mixture sticks together.

Knead very gently into a ball, and leave to rest for at least ½ hour, longer if possible. Take care not to over-handle, as, being such a rich dough, the butter will tend to become oily. The mixture can be frozen, but when required it must be at room temperature before using.

To make the filling, put the cottage cheese and single [light] cream into a food blender and mix together until smooth. Add the remainder of the ingredients and blend again until the mixture is creamy.

Roll out the pastry and cut into rings, put into a cake tin and spoon in the mixture. Cook in a hot oven for about 10 minutes; the time depends on the size of the tins chosen.

Serve hot straight from the oven or keep warm until required. A spoonful of clotted or double [heavy] cream on top to decorate is delicious.

The cheese pastry can also be made into small cheese biscuits, or a different flavoured pie crust. If making biscuits, roll out the pastry, cut into the desired shapes, place on a greased baking tray and cook in the oven at 200°C/400°F/Gas Mark 6, until just turning pale brown. Do not over-cook or the pastry will become bitter to the taste.

MOLASSES SPICED BEEF IN BEER

This dish comes from the North country, and can be happily bubbling and cooking away while you are out or entertaining. As in all dishes using beer, a good quality brew, full of flavour is the secret of a tasty and nourishing meal.

To serve 6–8

2 kg/4 lb piece of slow cooking cut of beef
    such as brisket, skirt etc.
1 kg/2 lb onions, peeled and sliced
1 litre /2 pints [5 cups] dark beer such as
    Theakston's 'Old Peculiar' or
    Wadworth's 'Old Timer'
For the marinade
125 g/4 oz [¼ cup] black treacle [molasses]
5 cloves
125 ml/¼ pint [½ cup] red wine vinegar
14 black peppercorns
1 tsp ground mace
pinch of salt
small clove garlic, crushed with a little salt
a bouquet garni

Combine all the ingredients for the marinade together in a large pan or bowl and place the beef in the liquid. Pile the sliced onion on top of the meat and leave in a cool place to marinade for at least 8 hours or overnight. Spoon the marinade over the beef from time to time.

Place the beef in a very large saucepan and pour in the marinade liquid and the onion. Pour in the beer, cover, and heat until almost boiling, then simmer very gently for about 3 to 3½ hours until the beef is tender.

Check the seasonings and serve with well-seasoned creamed potatoes or boiled potatoes, buttered carrots and green cabbage.

CIDER BAKED BRISKET OF BEEF

Now dear Nimrod adieu. Whenever you comes over to England, I shall be werry 'appy to see you in Great Coram-street, where dinner is on the table punctually at five on week days, and four on Sundays; and with best regards to Mrs Nimrod, and all the little Nimrods. I remain, for Self and Co., Yours to serve, John Jorrocks.

Jorrocks's Jaunts and Jollities,
R. S. Surtees, 1838

This brisket of beef would have been just the dinner enjoyed by Mr Jorrocks and Nimrod. It is served cold, so is ideal for a buffet or a picnic. A well hung piece of brisket is a must for this dish, so if possible, buy the beef at least two days before you start the recipe. Home-made bread and pickles are the traditional accompaniments to the beef.

To serve 6–8

2 kg/4 lb brisket of beef, soaked overnight
    in cold water approximately 4 days
    before required
1 onion, peeled and sliced
a bundle of fresh thyme, parsley,
    marjoram, tarragon etc.
2 carrots, peeled and cut into rings
16–20 black peppercorns
½ litre/1 pint [2½ cups] medium cider
½ litre/1 pint [2½ cups] boiling water
salt and pepper
1 tsp ground allspice
1 tsp cayenne pepper
10 cloves
1 tsp ground mace
1 tsp made mustard

Three days before required drain the beef from the salt water and place it into a large casserole along with the carrot and onion. Season well with the salt and pepper, add all the remaining spices and herbs. Pour in the cider and boiling water, cover, and cook in a pre-heated oven 130°C/250°F/Gas Mark ½ for 4 hours.

When ready, remove from the oven and allow the beef to cool in the liquid overnight.

The following day, remove the brisket and put it into a deep basin. Cover the beef with a plate or saucer that fits inside the rim of the basin, put a heavy weight on top and leave in a cool place until the following day.

When required, carve the brisket very thinly.

SHEPHERD'S PIE

In centuries past, the farms of some of the great Scottish landowners were of enormous extent. 'How many sheep have you on your estate?' asked Prince Esterhazy of the Duke of Argyll. 'I have not the most remote idea,' replied the duke; 'but I know the shepherds number several thousand.'

This dish is ideal for using up any left over meat; it is also warming, nourishing and delicious. This particular recipe was the favourite of the late Dorian Williams, when made by his wife. The secret of this dish is to make sure that you have a good flavoured gravy.

To serve 4

300 g/1 lb minced lamb or beef
2 medium sized onions, peeled and
     chopped
2 palms' full of peas
2 medium sized carrots, peeled and sliced
1 kg/2 lbs boiled potatoes ready for
     creaming
salt and ground black pepper
dripping [beef fat] for frying

Fry the onion and carrot together until the onion is just turning a golden brown. Remove from the pan.

Fry the minced meat until nicely browned. Remove from the pan and put with the onion and carrot. Mix these ingredients together along with the peas and place into a pie dish.

Make about 400 ml/¾ pint [2 cups] of gravy, using the residue of fat from the frying pan. The gravy must have a good strong flavour, if not, the pie will taste bland. Pour the gravy over the meat and season well.

Cream the potatoes, season well with ground black pepper and spread evenly over the top of the meat. Finish off by lining over the potato with a fork.

Put two dabs of butter on the top of the pie and place in the top of the oven for about 45 minutes at 375°F/190°C/Gas Mark 5. The potato should be a lovely golden brown.

IRISH BAKED HAM

Cooked in Guinness or dark beer, this delicious baked ham has a lovely mellow flavour which is characteristic of this Irish recipe.

To serve 6–8

2 kg/4 lb joint gammon ham [smoked
     shoulder roll]
60 g/2 oz [¼ cup] brown sugar
2 tsp brandy
125 ml/¼ pint [½ cup] Guinness or dark
     beer
60 g/2 oz [4 tbsp] butter
ground black pepper
1 tsp ground mace
½ litre/1 pint [2½ cups] cider
Parsley and watercress to decorate

Put the ham into a large saucepan and cover with water. Soak overnight. Drain off the water and rinse the ham.

Put the ham back into the saucepan and pour in the cider. If this does not cover the ham, add sufficient water to just cover. Sprinkle in the mace and pepper to taste and bring to the boil, cover, and simmer for 1½ hours.

When cooked, remove from the pan and strip off the rind. Mix the sugar, butter and brandy together and spread over the ham surface. Put the ham into an oven-proof dish and pour over the beer. Bake in the oven at 190°C/375°F/Gas Mark 5 for 30 minutes.

Serve hot or cold decorated with sprigs of fresh parsley or watercress.

PORK TENDERLOIN WITH MUSHROOMS

From Saxon times up until the First World War, nearly every countryman had a pig in the sty. There is an old saying that every part of the pig can be used except the squeak. He was so valuable an animal that he was often refered to as 'The Gentleman who paid the rent'. The most prized cut of the pig was the tenderloin. It seldom appeared for sale as the owner of the pig usually kept this tender cut of meat for himself and family.

To serve 4

250 g/8 oz mushrooms, wiped and finely
    chopped
1 kg/2 lb pork tenderloin, thinly sliced
    into about 12 pieces
150 g/5 oz [10 tbsp] unsalted butter
90 g/3 oz [6 tbsp] white breadcrumbs
salt and black pepper
2 tbsp chopped parsley
1 small clove garlic, crushed with a little
    salt
3 tbsp dry sherry
150 ml/$\frac{1}{4}$ pint [$\frac{1}{2}$ cup] double [heavy]
    cream
1 onion, peeled and finely chopped
2 tbsp oil
juice of $\frac{1}{2}$ lemon

Lay the pork pieces between two sheets of wet greaseproof [wax] paper and beat flat with a rolling pin. Put them into a dish with the oil, lemon juice, crushed garlic, salt and pepper, and marinade for about 30 minutes.

Meanwhile, melt the butter in a frying pan and gently cook the onion until soft but not brown, add the mushrooms and cook for a few minutes. Remove from the pan and keep warm.

Drain the pork pieces from the marinade and fry the meat in the butter for 3–4 minutes, turning once. Remove from the pan and keep warm.

Pour the sherry into the pan and stir over a high heat until reduced to about a tablespoon. Return the onion and mushrooms to the pan and season well. Stir in the cream and heat gently, stirring all the time until the liquid is almost boiling.

Remove the sauce from the heat and pour over the pork.

Quickly wipe the pan, add a little more butter and fry the breadcrumbs until golden brown in colour. Sprinkle them over the pork, sprinkle also the chopped parsley and serve at once.

Fried or boiled rice goes well with this dish if vegetables are not desired.

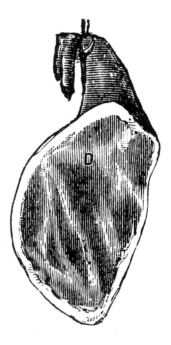

ROAST SADDLE OF LAMB

Never you mind about the piece of needlework, the tambouring and the maps of the world made by her needle. Get to see her at work upon a mutton chop, or a bit of bread and cheese, and, if she deal quickly with them, you have a pretty security for that activity, without which a wife is a burden instead of a help.

Advice to Young Men,
William Cobbett, 1829

Dorothy Hartley writes in her book *Food in England*, 'Saddle of mutton from the Welsh hills, or Scotland, is a joint for an epicure.' Mutton is not now so easily available, so we must use lamb. The saddle, being a fairly special joint of meat, makes the extra effort in cooking and preparing this dish, very worth while.

To serve 6–8

3 kg/6 lb saddle of lamb
4 tbsp medium sherry
4 tbsp brandy
1 bottle of good red wine
a good handful of fresh rosemary sprigs
4 tbsp redcurrant jelly
90 g/3 oz [scant ½ cup] dripping [beef fat]
2 onions, peeled and finely chopped
1 sprig thyme
1 carrot, peeled and finely chopped
8 black peppercorns
3 sprigs fresh chopped parsley
1 bay leaf
2 cloves
4 tbsp malt vinegar
1 blade of mace

Pre-heat the oven (after marinading) to 180°C/350°F/Gas Mark 4

Into a large pan put the chopped onion, rosemary sprigs, thyme, chopped carrot, peppercorns, cloves, parsley, mace, bay leaf and vinegar. Pour in 125 ml/¼ pint [½ cup] water and boil for 30 minutes. Allow to cool then stir in the wine, sherry and brandy. Put the lamb into the liquid and marinate for about 12 hours or overnight.

Remove the lamb from the marinade and put into a roasting dish. Dot over the dripping [beef fat]. Make small incisions in the meat and insert a few sprigs of fresh rosemary. Cook in the pre-heated oven for 2½ hours.

Meanwhile, quickly boil the marinade until reduced to about half the quantity. Strain the liquid and discard the herbs, bay leaf, spices and vegetable residue. Into the gravy, stir the redcurrant jelly and check the seasonings. If you like a thicker sauce, slacken 2 tsp of cornflour [cornstarch] with a little water and stir it into the gravy.

Serve with buttered new potatoes, baby carrots sprinkled with a little ground nutmeg and fresh orange juice, and broad beans.

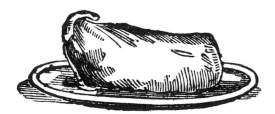

BOILED LEG OF MUTTON

This is capital mutton – never tasted better before . . . Mr Barnington, did you ever eat any Dartmoor mutton? It certainly is the best and sweetest in the world, and this is as like it as anything can possibly be . . .

> Captain Doleful at a dinner party
> given by Mr Barnington,
> from *Handley Cross*, R. S. Surtees, 1843

Sadly mutton is no longer the popular meat that it used to be, which is a pity as it is full of flavour and goodness. Those fortunate enough to have tasted mutton have said that it has far more flavour than a leg of lamb. Maybe it will become popular again one day; however, a leg of lamb is an adequate substitute.

To serve 8–10

1 leg of mutton or lamb
2 level tsp salt
2 onions, peeled and cut in half
4 whole carrots, peeled and sliced
2 sticks celery, washed and chopped
Water to cover

Trim the joint and remove any spare fat. Cooking time is 30 minutes to the $\frac{1}{2}$ kg/ 1 lb and 30 minutes over. If a leg of lamb, 20 minutes to the $\frac{1}{2}$ kg/1 lb, and 20 minutes over.

Put the mutton or lamb into a large saucepan with the water, add the salt and bring to the boil, skim off any scum, then add the vegetables, reduce the heat, cover and simmer until the meat is tender. Drain the liquid from the meat and serve.

If preferred, this dish can be eaten cold, served with home-made pickles and chutney.

MARBLED HAM

It is a pleasant, leisurely, business – this after-tea fishing. If you are fortunate you may get all your letters written beforehand: and if you are very fortunate you may even have paid all your bills. But before setting out a most important thing is to be sure that others will not wait dinner for you, to insist that a bit of cold meat, bread and cheese, is all you will require. If you feel at any time during the walk that you must hurry, then your evening is spoilt.

> *English Sport*,
> Captain H. F. H. Hardy, 1932

Originating from Yorkshire, this dish dates back to the eighteenth century. It was served at 'high teas' and parties. It is a very good way of using any leftover tongue or ham.

To serve 4–6

$\frac{1}{2}$ kg/1 lb cold minced ham
$\frac{1}{2}$ kg/1 lb cold minced tongue
$\frac{1}{4}$ tsp ground mace
$\frac{1}{4}$ kg/8 oz [1 cup] soft unsalted butter
ground black pepper
1 tbsp made mustard
clarified butter (see p. 16)

Pound the ham to a paste, beat in half the quantity of unsalted butter, season with half the mace and black pepper. Mix in half the quantity of mustard.

In a separate bowl, pound the tongue

to a paste, mix in the remaining unsalted butter, season with the mace, pepper and the remaining mustard.

Spread a thick layer of ham paste over the bottom of a deep basin or soufflé dish. Dot knobs of tongue paste over the ham, then another layer of ham paste spread over, then another layer of tongue paste knobs. Finish with a last layer of ham paste.

Cover with greaseproof [wax] paper, and weigh down with weights or other suitable heavy object. Allow to chill in the refrigerator overnight.

Remove the weights and paper and seal the top with clarified butter. Put back into the refrigerator to get very cold before serving.

Serve cut into wedge-shaped pieces with home-made bread and a fresh green salad.

ESCALOPES [SCALLOPINE] OF VEAL

Veal in England was practically unheard of until the conquering Normans demanded this unusual white meat. The Saxons would not slaughter a calf unless there was something wrong with it and this suspicion of veal continued right through the Middle Ages. The 'Blancmange' in the old cookery books was the white meat dressed in milk.

With the specialising of dairying in the eighteenth century, and with the new French fashion, veal recipes are found more often, but it is not a typical English meat; it is really a dish of Northern Italy, and when served with buttered pasta, it becomes a truly Italian traditional dish.

To serve 4

4 veal escalopes [scallopine]
180 g/6 oz [¾ cup] unsalted butter
250 g/½ lb button mushrooms
a little seasoned flour
1 tbsp olive oil
300 ml/½ pint [1¼ cups] chicken stock
150 ml/¼ pint [½ cup] medium sherry
150 ml/¼ pint [½ cup] double [heavy] cream

Beat the escalopes until thin and flat, coat them with the seasoned flour.

Heat the olive oil and 60 g/2 oz [¼ cup] of the butter in a heavy based saucepan, and fry the veal over a low heat for 4 minutes on each side. Remove from the heat and keep warm.

Slice the mushrooms and add to the pan along with the remaining butter, toss the mushrooms until well coated with butter and just turning a pale brown colour. Remove from the heat and keep warm.

Add the stock and sherry to the pan, stir and bring to the boil. Return the veal to the pan, lower the heat, cover, and simmer for 20 minutes, turning the meat once or twice so that it cooks evenly.

When cooked, arrange the veal on a hot serving dish and keep hot. Boil the juices in the pan until reduced by half and thickened slightly. Stir in the double [heavy] cream, remove from the heat and pour the sauce over the veal and mushrooms.

Garnish with sprigs of parsley and serve with buttered pasta, rice or fresh vegetables.

SAUTÉED LIVER WITH A PORT AND ORANGE SAUCE

'Nimrod' informs us that John Mytton, Esq. of Halston, Shropshire, drank from four to six bottles of port wine daily. The question of how did he consume this quantity is answered easily, Nimrod continues. He [John Mytton] shaved with a bottle of it on his toilet; he worked steadily at it throughout the day, by a glass or two at a time, and at least a bottle with his luncheon; and the after dinner and after supper work – not losing sight of it in the billiard room – completed the Herculean task.

The Life of John Mytton,
by Nimrod, 1837

I rather think that this dish would have gone down very well at Halston, providing that the cook could rescue a little port from the sideboard. I trust that you will not have that problem.

To serve 4

½ kg/1 lb lamb's liver
juice and rind [zest] of 2 small oranges
seasoned flour
60 g/2 oz [4 tbsp] unsalted butter
4 tbsp good port
125 ml/¼ pint [½ cup] brown gravy
    or stock
2 tsp redcurrant jelly
1 tbsp fresh chopped parsley
salt and black pepper

Cut the liver evenly into slices and remove any membranes or tubes. Toss the liver slices in the seasoned flour
    Melt the butter in a frying pan and quickly sauté the liver pieces until lightly brown. Pour in the stock, orange rind [zest], orange juice, port and redcurrant jelly. Simmer until the liver is tender.
    When cooked, remove the liver and keep warm. Boil up the juices in the pan until slightly reduced. Check the seasonings and pour over the liver. Sprinkle with the chopped parsley
    Serve with creamed potatoes, buttered carrots and runner beans.

SUPREME OF CHICKEN WITH BRANDY SAUCE

In a cold dark mediaeval night, groping for a fowl to cook for supper, you were instructed to 'take the one roosting next to the cock' – she was sure to be the fattest. Punctual-crowing cocks were genuinely useful on winter mornings. Giraldus Cambrensis notes with disapproval that cocks 'crow at a different time in Ireland'.

Food in England,
Dorothy Hartley, 1954

This recipe was kindly given to us by Steve and Clare Hadley. It is not only delicious, but also simple to make. It is a fairly rich dish, so keep accompanying vegetables simple.

To serve 4

4 chicken breasts
1 tbsp oil
125 g/¼ lb mushrooms, cleaned and sliced

90 g/3 oz [⅓ cup] unsalted butter
3 tbsp brandy
300 ml/½ pint [1¼ cups] double [heavy]
    cream
salt and pepper

Brush the chicken breasts with the oil,
season well and cook under a medium grill
[broiler] until cooked through and nicely
brown.

Melt the butter in a pan and cook the
mushrooms until tender. Increase the heat
and cook until the butter is dark brown,
then pour in the brandy and cream.

Boil rapidly, stirring all the time until
the sauce reduces to a coating consistency.
Adjust the seasonings and pour over the
chicken before serving.

HOT ARTICHOKE AND CHICKEN MOUSSE WITH ALMONDS

'Dinner will be served in a quarter of an
hour,' replied Walker. 'Dinner', exclaimed
Mr Jorrocks, looking at his watch; 'ten
minutes past seven, and not dined yet.
What will the world come to next? Dead
o'winter too.'

Handley Cross, R. S. Surtees, 1843

If this dish had been one of the courses, I
doubt if Mr Jorrocks would have minded
waiting too much, once he had begun the
meal that is. Any left over chicken meat
can be used for this recipe, but if you do
not have any, boneless breast of chicken
can be bought from most good
supermarkets or butchers.

To serve 6–8

180 g/6 oz artichoke pureé (350 g/¾ lb
    large artichokes, boiled, skin rubbed
    off and pureéd, should make the
    correct amount)
180 g/6 oz cooked chicken breast, finely
    minced
60 g/2 oz [4 tbsp] unsalted butter
45 g/1½ oz [scant ¼ cup] plain flour
100 ml/4 fl oz [½ cup] single [light] cream
    or milk
4 egg yolks
salt and black pepper
1 tbsp lightly toasted flaked almonds
5 egg whites
150 ml/¼ pint [⅔ cup] chicken stock

Pre-heat the oven to 200°C/400°F/Gas
Mark 6

Melt the butter in a large heavy-based
pan, stir in the flour and cook for a few
minutes. Add the chicken stock and mix
well until the liquid is sauce-like. Pour in
the cream or milk.

Remove from the heat and add the
minced chicken and artichoke pureé.
Whisk in the egg yolks one at a time.
Season to taste and add the toasted
almonds. Beat the egg whites then fold
them into the chicken and artichoke
mixture.

Grease a 1¼ litre/2½ pint soufflé dish.
Tie a double layer of buttered greaseproof
[wax] paper around the outside: the paper
should come up above the dish by about
4.5–6 cm/3–4 in.

Pour in the mousse mixture and bake
for 30–35 minutes until well risen and
golden brown, but still soft in the centre.
Remove the paper and string carefully and
serve immediately.

STELK
(A Potato and Spring Onion
[Scallion] Supper Dish)

A very good hot supper dish for a chilly
evening, and simple to prepare. Ordinary
onions can be used as an alternative to
spring onions [scallions], but it is the
green of the spring onion [scallion] that
helps to make this an attractive dish as
well as a delicious one. It is meant to be
eaten from the outside and dipping into
the pool of melted butter or bacon
dripping.

as many potatoes and spring onions
    [scallions] as you wish to serve
salt and black pepper
large lump of butter or bacon dripping
sufficient milk to cover the onion

Peel and boil the potatoes until cooked
and keep hot. Trim the onions [scallions]
and cut into small pieces.

    Put the milk into a saucepan and add
the chopped spring onion [scallions] and
simmer in the milk until tender.

    When cooked, remove the onion from
the milk, put to one side. Pour the onion-
flavoured milk into the drained, cooked
potato and cream together. Season very
well, especially with the pepper. Add the
chopped onion pieces, and mix well.

    Make a well in the centre of the potato
mound and put in the butter or bacon
dripping to melt.

    Sprinkle over with black pepper, and
grill [broil] for a couple of minutes to
brown the potato.

TROUT MOUSSE WITH A
WATERCRESS MAYONNAISE

Watercress is cultivated in clear, even-
flowing trout streams, the beds being
renovated each year in early autumn after
the cress has been harvested.

    This mousse is fairly simple to make,
and is ideal for a light lunch or supper
dish, or as a first course. It is also very
good to take on picnics, being easy to
transport.

To serve 4–6

½ kg/1 lb trout, poached, skin and bones
    removed
125 ml/¼ pint [½ cup] milk
300 ml/½ pint [1¼ cups] of the poaching
    liquid
3 level tsp plain [all purpose] flour
1 sprig fresh fennel or dill, chopped
1 tbsp anchovy essence [extract]
2 tsp tomato purée [paste]
juice of ½ lemon
1 tbsp sherry, medium
15 g/½ oz gelatine [unflavoured gelatin],
    dissolved in 4 tbsp warm water
125 ml/¼ pint [½ cup] double [heavy]
    cream
90 g/3 oz [6 tbsp] unsalted butter
For the mayonnaise
2 large bunches of watercress
300 ml/½ pint [1¼ cups] made mayonnaise
salt and black pepper

Mash the trout until smooth.

    Melt the butter in a saucepan, add the
flour and cook for 3 minutes stirring all
the time. Remove the pan from the heat
and add the poaching liquid. Gradually
stir in the milk. Add the chopped fennel or

dill, anchovy essence [extract], tomato pureé [paste], sherry, lemon juice. Pour in the dissolved gelatine. Whisk. Put to one side and allow to cool. Check seasoning.

When the sauce has cooled and is beginning to set, fold in the mashed trout. Beat the cream and fold into the mousse mixture. Put into individual pots or one large one and leave in a cool place until completely set.

For the watercress mayonnaise: wash and trim the watercress, reserve a few sprigs for decoration and steam the remainder for ten minutes. Rinse under cold water and chop or liquidize finely. Add the watercress to the mayonnaise and blend well and season to taste.

When required, decorate the trout mousse with twists of lemon and cucumber, plus sprigs of fresh herbs. Serve with the watercress mayonnaise and slices of thinly cut brown bread and butter.

CRUNCHY TROUT PIE

Crunchy trout pie is perfect for any traveller or sportsman coming home at the end of the day. It can be prepared in advance and put into the oven to heat through when required.

To serve 4

½ kg/1 lb trout, cooked, skin and bones removed
1 tin anchovy fillets, drained and soaked in 3 tbsp milk
60 g/2 oz [4 tbsp] unsalted butter
30 g/1 oz [2 tbsp] plain [all purpose] flour
300 ml /½ pint [1 cup] milk

2 level tsp tomato pureé [paste]
black pepper
4 tsp double [heavy] cream
90 g/3 oz [6 tbsp] wholemeal [whole wheat] breadcrumbs mixed with 3 tsp vegetable oil
1 onion, peeled and finely chopped
30 g/1 oz parsley, chopped

Put 30 g/1 oz [2 tbsp] of the butter into a pan and in it cook the onion until soft. Remove the onion from the pan and put on one side.

Melt the remaining butter in the pan and mix in the flour, cook for 2 minutes, gradually adding the milk and stirring well.

Return the cooked onion to the pan. Chop the soaked anchovies and add to the pan. Stir in the tomato pureé [paste] and black pepper.

Check the taste to see if the dish needs any salt. Take care with this, as the anchovies will be quite salty. Add the cream to the sauce mixture and sprinkle in the chopped parsley. Flake the trout meat and fold into the cream mixture.

Pour into an oven-proof dish. Top with the breadcrumbs and bake in the oven at 190°C/375°F/Gas Mark 5 for 30 to 35 minutes until the top is brown and crunchy. The cooking time may take a little longer if the mixture is cold when put into the oven.

WHITING AU GRATIN

The Victorians considered fish a wholesome food which is why it is so prolific on Victorian menus. For centuries it was thought to reduce the passions and so was encouraged by the early Christian church. 'Fyssche' days were observed up until the seventeenth century where Christians were not allowed to eat meat, as meat was thought to stimulate the passions.

The poorer people endured a monotonous diet of salt fish, whereas the rich enjoyed the better kinds of fish, such as sturgeon, pike, trout etc. Country estates as a rule had fish ponds or 'stews' in the grounds, well stocked with a variety of fresh fish.

To serve 4–5

4 whiting, cleaned, scaled, and heads removed
1 tbsp chopped parsley
125 g/4 oz mushrooms, cleaned and chopped
125 g/4 oz [½ cup] unsalted butter
salt and black pepper
2 glasses sherry (medium)
60 g/2 oz [¼ cup] breadcrumbs
60 g/2 oz [¼ cup] cheese, grated (Cheddar or Double Gloucester)

Grease the bottom of a baking dish and strew a few of the chopped mushrooms and a little parsley over the bottom. Lay the whiting in the dish and sprinkle over a little salt and pepper.

Mix the grated cheese with the breadcrumbs, then sprinkle over the fish. Add the remainder of the mushrooms and parsley. Pour in the sherry. Dot the butter over the fish and bake for 20 minutes in a hot oven 190°C/375°F/Gas Mark 5.

Should there be too much sauce for your liking, pour it off into a pan and reduce by boiling over a high heat for a few minutes until reduced by half.

Serve with wedges of lemon, a green salad and buttered new potatoes. Without the potatoes and salad, this dish will make an excellent first course.

SPICED SARDINE TOMATO CUPS

The tomato came to Europe from South America in the middle of the sixteenth century. It was thought to have been a good aphrodisiac, hence its original name of 'love apple'.

For this recipe, it is best to use one of the larger variety of tomato, such as the well flavoured 'Davington Epicure' or the big beefy tomato 'Big Boy' or 'Marmande'.

To serve 3–6

6 ripe tomatoes
2 hard boiled eggs
1 tin sardines
60 g/2 oz [4 tbsp] butter
1 tsp Dijon mustard
1 tsp cayenne pepper
2 tsp tarragon vinegar
salt and black pepper

Cut a piece off the top of each tomato to form a lid. If desired, use a star-shaped cutter to cut the lids into a fancy shape.

Scoop the pulp from the tomato, reserve in a bowl for the sauce. Dust the tomato cups with salt and turn them upside down on a wire rack to drain for about 20 minutes.

Remove the skin and bones from the sardines and mash them with the butter and the mustard. Sieve the egg yolks and mix into the sardine and butter mixture. Add the cayenne pepper and the seasonings. Chop the egg white and mix into the sardine filling mixture.

Put the filling into the tomato cups and place the lids on top. Chill before serving.

Sieve the scooped-out tomato pulp, pour in the tarragon vinegar. Season well. A little chopped herb mixture can be added if desired.

When ready to serve, spoon the sauce over each tomato cup and sprinkle over finely chopped parsley.

CRAB MOUSSE WITH AVOCADO SAUCE

Buy my flounders; twelve pence a peck;
Crab, crab, any crab,
Hot baked wardens, all fresh and fair.
          Pedlars' and Market Cries, London

To serve 6–8

350 g/¾ lb cream cheese (e.g. Philadelphia)
1 tin 425 ml/15 fl oz good quality crab
    soup
2 tbsp mayonnaise
juice of 2 small lemons
4 tsp gelatine [unflavoured gelatin]

500 g/1 lb [2 cups] crab meat, white and
    brown
300 ml/½ pint] [1¼ cups] double [heavy]
    cream
salt and black pepper
For the sauce
1 large ripe avocado, peeled and chopped
juice of 1½ lemons
a little sugar, about 2 tsp
300 ml/½ pint [1¼ cups] double [heavy]
    cream
salt and white pepper
slices of lemon and cucumber to garnish

Put the mayonnaise, soup, lemon juice, cream cheese and seasonings into a liquidizer and blend until smooth. Pour into a large bowl.

Dissolve the gelatine in a small cup with four tbsp of cold water by standing the small cup in a pan of hot water. Pour the dissolved gelatine into the cream cheese and soup mixture, whisking all the time.

Whip the double [heavy] cream until it just begins to thicken, and fold into the mousse mixture gently. Mix in the crab meat and check the seasonings. Put into a dish or mould, allow to set.

To make the sauce, put all the ingredients into a liquidizer and blend until the mixture is smooth. This must be done at the last moment to retain the delicate green colour. Check the seasonings.

When required, unmould the crab mousse onto a serving dish and pour over the avocado sauce (or it can be served separately).

Decorate with the cucumber and lemon slices and a few sprigs of fresh parsley if desired.

31

FISHERMAN'S HOT POT

But yet, though while I fish, I fast,
I make good fortune my repast;
And thereunto my friend invite,
In whom I more than that delight:
Who is more welcome to my dish
Than to my angle was my fish.

The Angler's Song,
William Basse (1602–1653)

This is a wonderful dish to come home to after a cold, wet day's fishing. In this recipe, cod fillets are used, though any white fish of your choice can be substituted. It is a good way of using any left over fish and small pieces of cheese, though the cheese must be a good flavoured variety.

To serve 4

500 g/1 lb cod fillet
750 g/1½ lb potatoes, peeled
2 tbsp lemon juice
45 g/1½ oz [3 tbsp] plain flour
1 onion, peeled and thinly sliced
250 g/8 oz mushrooms, cleaned and sliced
150 ml/¼ pint [½ cup] milk
15 g/½ oz [1 tbsp] unsalted butter
125 g/4 oz [good cup] Cheddar cheese,
    grated
salt and black pepper

Remove any skin from the fillets of cod and cut the fish into squares, toss in 25 g/1 oz [¼ cup] of the flour.

Put the potatoes into a saucepan and boil until just tender, not too soft. Slice thinly and arrange one-third on the bottom of a buttered casserole dish. Cover with half the amount of cod, pour over the lemon juice and season well.

In a frying pan, fry the onion for a couple of minutes until it just begins to change colour, then remove from the pan. Combine the cooked onion with the mushroom slices and arrange half the mixture over the fish. Cover with the remaining cod and a little more seasoning. Put in another third of the amount of the sliced potato and the remaining onion and mushrooms.

Melt the butter in a frying pan and stir in the remaining flour, cook for one minute. Remove the pan from the heat and gradually add the milk, stirring all the time. Bring to the boil then cook until the sauce begins to thicken, again stirring all the time.

Add half the quantity of cheese to the sauce and season well. Pour the mixture over the casserole ingredients, arrange the remaining potato slices on top, sprinkle over the last of the cheese and bake in the oven, without a lid, for 40 minutes or until the top is golden brown, at 200°C/400°F/Gas Mark 6.

LOBSTER THERMIDOR

From his North country seat at Alnwick Castle, the Duke of Northumberland very kindly gave this recipe for his favourite dish. The county of Northumberland has a reputation for breeding famous and hardy sportsmen: men like the mild-mannered and courteous Ralph Lambton, MFH, and his neighbour, the great sporting writer, Robert Smith Surtees, himself a very capable Master of Fox Hounds, who practised the true science of venery in this rough country.

To serve 2 as a main course,
4 as a first course

2 small cooked lobsters
pinch paprika
2 tbsp tarragon, chopped
60 g/2 oz [4 tbsp] unsalted butter
1 small shallot, peeled and chopped
2 tsp parsley, chopped
4 tbsp dry white wine
3 tbsp Parmesan cheese, grated
300 ml/½ pint [1¼ cup] béchamel sauce
salt and black pepper

Remove the lobster meat from the shell, chop the meat into small pieces.

Melt 30 g/1 oz [2 tbsp] of the butter in a saucepan, add the tarragon, parsley and shallot, stir and cook for 2 minutes, then add the wine and simmer for 5 minutes. Add the béchamel sauce, and simmer until reduced to a creamy texture.

Put the lobster meat into this sauce, sprinkle in two tbsp of the grated cheese. Add the remaining butter, paprika, salt and pepper. A little mustard can be added if desired at this stage.

Arrange the mixture onto a warm serving dish, or if you prefer, back into the lobster shell. Sprinkle over the remaining spoonful of grated Parmesan cheese and pop under a hot grill just long enough to brown the cheese.

Decorate with sprigs of fresh parsley and serve with a fresh green salad.

SAUCE À LA REFORM

Alexis Soyer, the most celebrated cook of his period, was renowned for his culinary exploits at the new Reform Club in Pall Mall. On one great occasion, he prepared a banquet for twelve hundred people which had been so lavish that the scraps provided a meal for seven hundred paupers the next day. He was, in fact, a great friend to the poor in Ireland and London for whom he organised soup kitchens and devised cheap and nourishing recipes.

For many years Alexis Soyer reigned over the palates and stomachs of the Liberal aristocracy. Here is his famous sauce which is a marvellous accompaniment to all kinds of game or meat.

(I am indebted to the members of the Reform Club for their help with my research, particularly Mr E. J. Aaronson who very kindly loaned me the limited edition of *The Selected Soyer*.)

Cut up two middling-sized onions into thin slices and put them into a stewpan with two sprigs of parsley, two of thyme, two bay leaves, two ounces of lean uncooked ham, half a clove of garlic, half a blade of mace, and an ounce of fresh butter; stir them ten minutes over a sharp fire, then add two tablespoonfuls of Tarragon vinegar, and one of chili vinegar, boil for one minute; then add a pint of brown sauce, or sauce Espagnole, three tablespoons of preserved tomatoes, and eight of consommé; place it over the fire until boiling, then put it at the corner, let it simmer ten minutes, skim it well, then place it again over the fire, keeping it stirred, and reduce until it adheres to the back of the spoon; then add a good tablespoonful of redcurrant jelly, and half doz. of chopped mushrooms; season a little more if required with pepper and salt; stir it until the jelly is melted, then pass it through a tammie [triangular fine strainer] into another stewpan. When ready to serve, make it hot, and add the white of a hard-boiled egg cut into strips half an inch long, and thick in proportion, four white blanched mushrooms, one gherkin, two green Indian pickles, and half an ounce of cooked ham, or tongue, all cut in strips like the white of egg; do not let it boil afterwards. This sauce must be poured over whatever it is served with.

From *The Selected Soyer*, compiled by Andrew Langley, 1837

CHOCOLATE MINT MOUSSE

Charles and Tom Palmer walked over from Eardisley to see me. The day was bitterly cold with a cruel East wind and whilst they were here a wild snowstorm came on.

Kilvert's Diary, 30 March 1878

That sounds like a fairly typical March day when no sport of any kind is to be had. Just right for staying by the fire and enjoying lunch or supper with friends. This mousse is especially good for an 'at home' day. Very rich and dark, it makes an excellent pudding.

To serve 4–6

500 g/2 large bars dark plain [semi-sweet]
    chocolate
3 eggs, separated
60 g/2 oz [4 tbsp] unsalted butter
4 tsp coffee essence [extract]
3 tbsp water
2 tsp peppermint essence [extract]
90 g/3 oz whipping cream
a few chocolate mints for decoration
whipping cream for decoration

Break the chocolate into small pieces and
put it into a large bowl. Add the 3 tbsp
water, coffee essence [extract], butter and
peppermint essence [extract]. Stand the
bowl over a pan of hot water; the water
should not touch the bottom of the bowl
— if it does, it will overheat the chocolate.

Stir all the ingredients well until free of
lumps and the mixture is thick and glossy.
Whisk in the egg yolks one at a time; this
must be done over the heat.

When completely blended, remove the
bowl from the heat and allow the mixture
to cool. The bowl can be suspended over
another bowl full of iced water.

While the chocolate is cooling, whip
the cream and whisk the egg whites to a
'snow'. When the mousse is cold, fold in
the whipped cream and the egg white.

Pour the mousse into a large serving
bowl or individual bowls and put in the
refrigerator to set.

When required, take the mousse from
the refrigerator, whip the cream set aside
for decoration, and with a star nozzle,
pipe cream rosettes onto the mousse. Put
one or two chocolate mints in the centre,
more if you prefer.

HAZELNUT MERINGUE GATEAU

To serve 4–6

125 g/4 oz [½ cup] shelled hazelnuts,
    toasted and pounded into small pieces
250 g/8 oz [1 cup] caster [superfine] sugar
4 large egg whites
250 g/8 oz [1 cup] whipping cream
icing [confectioner's] sugar to taste

Whisk the egg whites until they are very
stiff. Fold in the caster sugar a spoonful at
a time, then fold in the crushed hazelnuts.
Do this gently so as not to over mix.

Divide the mixture between two trays
that have been lined with non-stick baking
paper. Spread the meringue mixture into
a circle with a palette knife. Put into the
bottom of the oven at its lowest
temperature, about 100°C/200°F/the
lowest the gas will go without going out.
Allow the meringue to dry out for 3–4
hours then turn off the oven and allow the
gateau to cool in the oven.

When cold, remove the gateau from
the oven, peel away the baking paper.
Whip the cream and sandwich the two
halves of meringue together with the
cream. Dust over with the icing
[confectioner's] sugar and decorate with a
little fresh fruit if you have any.

This gateau can be served with a fresh
fruit pureé such as raspberry or
strawberry.

NORWEGIAN CREAM WITH CARAQUE CHOCOLATE

This delicious sweet is an elaborate way of serving the traditional egg custard. Custard had its heyday in the Victorian era when it almost invariably accompanied other puddings on the menu. It was served in small glass custard cups.

To serve 4

2 large tsp apricot jam
3 eggs and 1 egg white
3 tsp sugar
$\frac{1}{2}$ tsp vanilla essence [extract]
400 ml/$\frac{3}{4}$ pint [2 cups] hot milk
6 tbsp double [heavy] or whipping cream
caraque chocolate (approx 200 g/7 oz)

To make the caraque chocolate, melt sufficient chocolate to your requirements into a bowl which has been placed over a saucepan half filled with hot water. Spread the melted chocolate onto a marble slab and allow to cool.

Take a pallet knife and gently scrape the chocolate off the slab, using a sawing action. It should come off in long rolls of chocolate. If if does not, it is not too drastic, as chocolate shavings look equally attractive.

To make the cream, spread the jam over the bottom of a soufflé dish. Break 3 eggs into a bowl and whisk together with the sugar and vanilla essence [extract]. Pour in the hot milk and blend in well. Strain into the soufflé dish.

Stand the dish in a tin half full of hot water. Cover the dish with greaseproof [wax] paper and put into a moderate oven. Cook until firm to the touch. Leave to one side until cold.

Whip the cream and the remaining egg white separately, then blend together. Cover the custard in the soufflé dish with caraque chocolate, then pile the egg white and cream mixture on top. Decorate with a little more caraque chocolate. Serve at once.

RHUBARB AND GINGER FOOL

All things that love the sun are out of
doors;
The sky rejoices in the morning's birth;
The grass is bright with rain-drops;
– on the moors
The hare is running races in her mirth;
And with her feet she from
the plashy earth
Raises a mist; that, glittering in the sun,
Runs with her all the way, wherever
she doth run.
Resolution and Independence,
William Wordsworth, 1807

To serve 6–8

750 g/1½ lb young rhubarb, washed,
trimmed, cut into pieces
juice and grated rind [zest] of 1 orange
4 tbsp honey or brown sugar
300 ml/½ pint [1¼ cups] double cream
4 pieces preserved ginger in syrup

Put the rhubarb pieces into a large pan,
add the honey or sugar, orange juice and
rind, cover, and cook over a low heat so
the rhubarb does not burn or stick to the
bottom of the pan. Stir from time to time.

When the rhubarb is ready put all the
ingredients from the pan into a liquidiser
and blend until smooth and creamy. Pour
out into a bowl and cool.

Beat the cream and fold into the
rhubarb pureé. Chop the ginger pieces and
fold these into the mixture.

Pile the fool into a glass bowl or
individual glasses and decorate with a
fresh orange segment; serve with a biscuit
of shortbread.

NEWMARKET SYLLABUB

. . . there is nothing more cheering to the
spirits, than the sight and air of
Newmarket Heath on a fine fresh spring
morning like the present. The wind seems
to go by you at a racing pace, and the
blood canters up and down the veins with
the finest and freest action imaginable.
Mr Jorrocks at Newmarket,
from *Jorrocks's Jaunts and Jollities*,
R. S. Surtees, 1838

To serve 6

½ litre/1 pint [2½ cup] double [heavy]
cream
300 ml /½ pint [1¼ cups] sweet white
dessert wine
¾ tbsp English honey
6 tbsp brandy

Put the wine, brandy and honey into a
bowl and blend the ingredients well
together. Gradually whip in the double
[heavy] cream. When the mixture is thick,
pour into a large glass bowl or six
individual glasses. A little nutmeg can be
sprinkled over if desired.

If a less sweet syllabub is required, a
little lemon juice can be added along with
the wine and brandy.

BEAVER HAT PUDDING

Squire, farmer, stage-coachman, innkeeper, traveller, labourer, gamekeeper, tinker, tailor, butcher, baker and candlestick maker – they all wore the beaver hat.

They wore it in love and in sport, in travel, and of course to church. They went shooting in it, they hunted in it, and fished and played cricket in it; and the only time they discarded it was when they went to bed – when they always put on a nightcap in case their heads should miss it.

The Romance of the Road,
Cecil Aldin, 1928

This delicious sponge pudding separates during cooking to give its own sauce. When the pudding is cooked and turned out for serving a good deep dish is necessary to catch the sauce.

To serve 4

250 g/8 oz [1 cup] **English butter**
360 g/12 oz [1½ cups] **soft brown sugar**
2 large eggs, beaten
250 g/4 oz [2 cups] **dark [semi-sweet] chocolate, melted in a pan over hot water**
¼ kg/8 oz [2 cups] **self-raising flour [cake flour plus 1½ tsp baking powder]**
½ litre/1 pint [2¼ cups] **milk**
60 g/2 oz **chopped walnuts (optional)**

Beat the butter and ¼ kg/8 oz [1¼ cups] of the sugar together. Gradually beat in the eggs. Beat in the melted chocolate. Fold in the flour and walnuts if used.

When all the ingredients have been thoroughly combined, pour the mixture into a 2 litre /4 pint greased oven-proof basin or dish. Mix together the remaining sugar with the milk and pour over the sponge mixture.

Put into the oven and bake at 170°C/ 325°F/Gas Mark 3, for 1 hour 25 minutes, until the pudding is spongy to the touch.

When ready, run a palette knife around the edge of the pudding to loosen away from the basin and turn out onto your serving dish.

ICED GOOSEBERRY FOOL

That thither all the season did pursue
Wi'mellow goosberrys of every hue

The Shepherd's Calendar,
John Clare, 1827

The gooseberry is one of the first fruits of spring, and one which grew prolifically in old cottage or farmhouse kitchen gardens. With a tartness and a flavour all of their own, the small, green gooseberry is ideal for fools, mousses, and other puddings.

To serve 4–6

500 g/1 lb **gooseberries, washed, topped and tailed (reserve 2 for decoration)**
300 ml/½ pint [1¼ cups] **double [heavy] or single [light] cream, or half the amount of each**
125–180 g/4–6 oz [½–¾ cup] **sugar, amount depending on taste**

Put the gooseberries into a pan with a little water, or a little butter if preferred, and simmer until the fruit is soft (about 5 to 8 minutes).

Remove the fruit from the pan and rub through a sieve into a bowl. Stir in the sugar, enough to your taste. Allow to cool.

Whip the cream until it just holds its shape, fold into the pureé. Pile into a serving dish and chill for several hours.

When required, decorate with one or two gooseberries cut in half, and a small fresh flower, pink if possible to complement the delicate green colour of the fool.

GOOSEBERRY AND HONEY PIE

Green gooseberries. Lapwings' eggs at the poulterers.

Journals, Gilbert White,
8 May 1769

Gooseberries have been featured in English cooking over since Tudor times; nearly every cottage garden grew its own gooseberry bush. It was favoured, not just because it was an easy fruit to grow, but also because of its wide versatility in cooking, savoury as well as sweet. The addition of honey helps to offset the tartness of the gooseberry in this recipe; more or less honey can be added according to preference.

To serve 4–6

3 tbsp honey
60 g/2 oz [¼ cup] soft brown sugar
750 g/1½ lb gooseberries, topped and
    tailed
60 g/2 oz [4 tbsp] unsalted butter
4 tbsp fresh orange juice
milk to glaze
unrefined golden granulated sugar to
    sprinkle
250 g/8 oz prepared shortcrust [pie] pastry

Place a pie funnel in a deep pie dish (about 1 litre/2 pint). Put the prepared gooseberries into the dish and sprinkle over the brown sugar, dot the fruit with the butter. Pour in the orange juice and honey.

Roll the pastry to form a lid. Moisten the rim of the dish. Cut a strip of pastry from the pastry round and press this around the edge of the pie dish. Cover the whole with the remaining pastry lid and seal well. Flute the edges and brush over with the milk.

Sprinkle over a little golden sugar and bake in a hot oven for 20 minutes, 220°C/425°F/Gas Mark 7. Then reduce the temperature to 200°C/400°F/Gas Mark 6 and cook for a further 20 minutes.

When ready, sprinkle with a little more sugar and serve with clotted or double [heavy] cream.

OLD ENGLISH SHERRY TRIFLE

Give me sacke, old sacke, boys,
To make the muses merry,
The life of mirth and the joy of the earth
Is a cup of good old sherry.
> Ballad from Pasquil's Palinodia,
> *Inns, Ales, and drinking customs*
> *of old England,*
> F. W. Hackwood, 1851

To serve 8–10

For the trifle
500 g/1 lb plain sponge cake
125 g/4 oz [⅓ cup] raspberry or strawberry
    jam, home-made if possible
100 ml/4 fl oz [½ cup] dry sherry
100 ml/4 fl oz [½ cup] brandy, optional
180 g/6 oz [¾ cup] flaked almonds, toasted
2 tbsp caster [superfine] sugar
500 g/1 lb fresh or tinned raspberries
300 ml/½ pint [1¼ cups] whipping cream
For the custard topping
400 ml/¾ pint [2 cups] milk
½ vanilla pod [bean]
3 tbsp caster [superfine] sugar
7 egg yolks
125 ml/¼ pint [½ cup] double [heavy]
    cream
2 pkts (15 g/½ oz sachets) gelatine
    [unflavoured gelatin]

Slice the sponge cake to the thickness of a
thick slice of toast. Line a bowl with the
cake slices, spread over the jam, and pour
over the sherry, and brandy if used. Make
sure the cake is well soaked with the wine.
Scatter half the quantity of almonds over
the cake and pour in the raspberries.

    To make the custard: heat the milk
with the vanilla pod [bean] and allow to
infuse for 20 minutes.

    Whisk the egg yolks and sugar
together until thick and creamy. After the
20 minutes, remove the vanilla pod from
the milk and pour the warm milk over the
egg mixture. Strain this mixture into a
clean saucepan and heat gently, stirring
constantly, until it just begins to thicken,
remove from the heat.

    Soften the gelatine in a little cold
water, then whisk into the custard. Allow
to cool.

    Whisk in the double [heavy] cream,
then pour the custard over the sponge and
raspberries. Cover, and allow to cool
completely and set.

    When the custard has set, whisk the
whipping creamy and caster [superfine]
sugar together and spread or pipe over the
top of the custard. Scatter the remaining
almonds over the top.

QUEEN OF PUDDINGS

A sporting young man and his elderly
mother from the country were attending a
race meeting; it was the old lady's first
experience of racing. 'I say, mother,' said
the young man, 'I've been wondering for
ages what's in the bulky parcel you're
carrying.' 'Well,' said the old lady, 'in
your letter you said to bring something to
put on the horses . . . so I brought this old
eiderdown, I hope it isn't too shabby.'
> *Sporting and Dramatic Yarns,*
> R. J. B. Sellar, 1925

Elderly mothers may not be too
conversant with the rules of horse racing,
but they would certainly be familiar with
this 'queen of puddings'. Though a

spectacular pudding with its golden brown meringue topping, it is very simple to make.

To serve 4–6

grated rind [zest] of 1 lemon or 2 limes
4 large egg yolks
150 g/5 oz [1 cup] fine white breadcrumbs
60 g/2 oz [4 tbsp] vanilla or caster [superfine] sugar
60 g/2 oz [¼ cup] butter
½ litre/1 pint [2½ cups] creamy milk
3 tbsp raspberry or strawberry jam (home-made if possible)
3 tbsp lemon curd if using limes
For the topping
4 egg whites
180 g/6 oz [¾ cup] caster [superfine] sugar

Mix together the breadcrumbs and the sugar, stir in the lime or lemon rind [zest].

Pour the milk into a saucepan and heat until just warm. Add the butter and allow to melt, whisk in the egg yolks and pour over the breadcrumb and sugar mixture.

Put the mixture into a dish or soufflé bowl and leave for 30 minutes to allow the breadcrumbs to swell in the milk. After that time, bake in the oven for 30 minutes at 180°C/350°F/Gas Mark 4. The top should be firm to the touch when ready.

When the mixture has set, spread the jam or curd evenly over the top taking care not to break the surface crust.

Beat the egg whites until very stiff, add the sugar a spoon at a time, gradually folding in until all is thoroughly blended.

Spread the meringue mixture over the jam surface and make the meringue into 'peaks'. Dust over a little more caster [superfine] sugar and return to the oven to lightly brown the meringue. The oven can be turned off and the pudding left in until required. This will help in crisping the meringue, and prevent over-browning.

IRISH WHISKEY LEMON CAKE

The first delicate pangs of hunger were stealing upon us, and I felt reasonably certain that nothing necessary to our welfare had been forgotten. I lit a cigarette and pulled my cap over my eyes, and listened to a lark, spiring, like the smoke, into the blue, while my wife clattered in the luncheon basket. It was a moment of entire well-being, overshadowed only by the prospect of having to take an interest in the racing.

In Mr Knox's Country,
Somerville and Ross, 1915

To serve 6

6 tbsp Irish Whiskey
180 g/6 oz [¾ cup] softened butter
180 g/6 oz [1 cup] sultanas [golden raisins]
finely grated rind [zest] and juice of 1 large
    lemon
3 eggs, separated
180 g/6 oz [¾ cup] caster [superfine] sugar
125 g/4 oz [1 cup] self-raising flour, sifted
    [cake flour plus ¾ tsp baking powder]
60 g/2 oz [½ cup] ground almonds
For the icing
125 g/4 oz [1 cup] icing [confectioner's]
    sugar
juice of ½ lemon
a little Irish Whiskey, sufficient to mix to
    a coating consistency

Into a bowl, put the sultanas [golden raisins], lemon rind [zest] and juice, and the whiskey. Leave overnight to soak

The next day, cream the sugar and butter together until fluffy and light. One at a time, beat in the egg yolks along with a spoonful of flour. Add the sultanas,

lemon rind [zest] and the soaking liquid and mix well with the remaining flour and ground almonds.

Whisk the egg whites until stiff and fold into the flour and almond mixture. Turn the mixture into a greased and lined cake tin, about 20 cm/8 in square. Bake in a moderate oven 160°C/325°F/Gas Mark 3 for 1½ hours, until firm to the touch.

When cooked, allow to cool. Mix the icing sugar, lemon juice and the whiskey until it is a coating consistency, and spread over the top of the cake.

SEED CAKE

I saw Mrs Jamieson eating seed-cake, slowly and considerately, as she did everything; and I was rather surprised, for I knew she had told us, on the occasion of her last party, that she never had it in her house, it reminded her so much of scented soap. She always gave us Savoy biscuits. However, Mrs Jamieson was kindly indulgent to Miss Barker's want of knowledge of the customs of high life; and, to spare her feelings, ate three large pieces of seed-cake, with a placid, ruminating expression of countenance, not unlike a cow's.

Cranford, Elizabeth Gaskell, 1853

Seed-cake was a great tea-time favourite during the eighteenth century. With its distinctive flavour of caraway seeds, it not only goes well with tea, but also with a glass of sweet wine or sherry.

To serve 4–6

125 g/4 oz [½ cup] butter
2 eggs, beaten
1 heaped tsp caraway seeds
125 g/4 oz [½ cup] caster [superfine] sugar
180 g/6 oz [1½ cups] self-raising flour
   [cake flour plus 1 tsp baking powder],
   sifted
30 g/1 oz [2 tbsp] mixed chopped peel
1 tbsp warm water

Pre-heat the oven to 180°C/350°F/Gas
   Mark 4

Cream the sugar and butter together. Add
the beaten egg a little at a time. Beat in
well. Stir in the sifted flour, caraway seeds
and mixed peel. Pour in the water and mix
well.

Spoon into a greased, lined cake tin
and smooth the top. Sprinkle over a few
extra caraway seeds and bake for one
hour.

DARK RUM BUTTER CAKE

Gobble, gobble, gobble, was the order of
the day.

Mr Sponge's Sporting Tour,
R. S. Surtees, 1853

To serve approximately 6

180 g/6 oz [¾ cup] unsalted butter
5 eggs
1 tsp baking powder
225 g/7 oz [1 cup] caster [superfine] sugar
90 g/3 oz [scant ½ cup] semolina
4 tbsp dark rum
grated rind [zest] and juice of 1 lemon
grated rind [zest] and juice of 1 orange
275 g/9 oz [2 cups] self-raising flour [cake
   flour plus 1½ tsp baking powder]

Pre-heat the oven to 190°C/375°F/Gas
   Mark 5

Grease a 1 kg/2 lb loaf tin, sprinkle the
inside with flour.

Beat the sugar and butter together
until pale and creamy. Add the eggs one
at a time.

Sift the semolina, flour and baking
powder together and fold gently into the
egg mixture.

Gradually add the orange and lemon
juice, the rum and the grated orange and
lemon rind [zest].

Blend gently and well. Pour the
mixture into the prepared tin, smooth the
top and bake for 1¼ hours. Cover with foil
if the top is turning very brown. Turn out
onto a wire rack and allow to cool.

The top can be decorated, if desired,
by a rum-flavoured icing.

FRUIT AND ALMOND CAKE

To serve 8–10

½ kg/1 lb [2 cups] unsalted butter
½ kg/1 lb [2 cups] caster [superfine] sugar
grated rind [zest] of one lemon
8 eggs
2 tsp mixed spice
600 g/1¼ lb [5 cups] plain [all purpose]
    flour
1 tsp baking powder
¾ kg/1½ lb [5 cups] sultanas [golden
    raisins]
125 g/¼ lb [½ cup] mixed peel
60 g/2 oz [¼ cup] split and blanched
    almonds

Cream together the butter and sugar, add
the grated lemon rind [zest]; then one by
one beat in the eggs. Beat all for 10
minutes then work in the flour, mixed
spice and baking powder. Mix in the
sultanas [golden raisins] and mixed peel.

Put the mixture into a buttered cake
tin and decorate the top with the blanched
almonds arranged in circles and pushed
into the mixture. Bake in a moderate oven
for 2½ hours.

Lady Jekyll's Kitchen Essays, 1921

RHUBARB, FIG AND GINGER JAM

Preserved ginger comes to us from the
West Indies, and is made by scalding the
roots when they are still green, peeling

them in cold water, and putting them into
jars with a rich syrup. Good ginger should
have a bright colour and have a little
transparency about it. It should not be
dark or fibrous.

This jam combines very different
textures and flavours, but they blend well
together to make a delicious and unusual
preserve, especially when spread upon a
thick slice of home-made bread and good
English butter.

To make approximately 4 kg/8 lb

1 litre/2 pints [5 cups] water
¾ kg/1½ lb dried figs
¼ kg/½ lb preserved ginger
1 kg/2 lb rhubarb, cleaned and trimmed
grated rind [zest] and juice of 2 oranges
2½ kg/5 lb [10 cups] preserving sugar

The day before your jam making, cut the
figs into pieces and soak in the water
overnight.

Cut the rhubarb into small pieces and
put into a preserving pan. Pour in the
water, add the figs and bring to the boil.
Simmer until very soft.

Remove from the heat and stir in the
sugar and orange juice and rind [zest].
Keep stirring until the sugar has dissolved.

Return the pan to the heat and boil
rapidly, stirring from time to time to
prevent sticking. Skim if necessary. Add
the preserved ginger with a little of the
syrup if desired. Mix well.

Test for setting by putting a little jam
onto a saucer, allow to cool.

When a set has been obtained, stir
once more to separate any fruit lumps and
put into clean jam pots. Cover, and seal
well.

JAM TARTS

'Yes indeed,' Master Tate says: 'I could eat something. I could eat ten million jam tarts covered with buckets of custard.'
Coaching Days of Old England, 1966

Elizabethan cooks would boil up highly spiced fruit to make a thick purée, and fill tarts with this spiced fruit, which would go to table along with the savoury dishes. They were served as part of the same course from medieval times until the eighteenth century; diners would select what took their fancy from the range of dishes. Sweet tarts and pies became popular from the seventeenth century when sugar became cheaper and more widely available. This resulted in the decline in the use of spices.

Jam tarts can be eaten hot or cold, but there is not much to beat home-made tarts straight from the oven bubbling with home-made jam.

To make 6–8 small tarts
jam, flavour according taste
250 g/8 oz shortcrust [pie] pastry

Pre-heat the oven 375°F/190°C/Gas Mark 5

Roll out the pastry, cut out the selected number of rings; put each pastry ring into a tart tin.

Put the jam into each tart; do not overfill, or it will boil over and cover the tart.

Put into a pre-heated oven and cook for 10–12 minutes, taking care not to over cook or the jam will caramelize and burn.

If one tart is turned upside down and put with another so the jam is in the centre, they can be taken in your pocket when out riding, hunting or just walking.

DARK OATY SLICES

These delicious oat slices are ideal for a simple or a high tea. They can be taken on picnics, or put into ones pocket when out for a day's sport. The flavour improves with keeping, so store for several days before cutting.

To make approximately 12 cakes
125 g/4 oz [2 cups] rolled oats
125 g/4 oz [1 cup] self-raising flour [cake flour plus $\frac{3}{4}$ tsp baking powder]
125 g/4 oz [$\frac{1}{4}$ cup] black treacle [molasses]
9 tbsp oil
125 g/4 oz [$\frac{1}{2}$ cup] demerara sugar
1 egg, beaten with 4 tbsp milk

Grease and line the base of a 18 cm/7 in square tin.

Put the oats and flour into a bowl. Gently warm the treacle, oil and sugar in a pan until the sugar has dissolved. Make a well in the centre of the oats and flour and pour in the egg and milk, then the dissolved oil, treacle and sugar syrup. Beat well for a couple of minutes, pour into the tin and bake in the centre of the oven for 1–1¼ hours at 160°C/325°F/Gas Mark 3. Allow to cool on a wire tray and store in an air-tight tin for one week.

SUMMER

An inward love breeds outward talk,
The hound some praise, and some the hawk;
Some, better pleased with private sport,
use tennis; some a mistress court:
But their delights I neither wish,
Nor envy, while I freely fish.
English Sport, Captain H. F. H. Hardy, 1932

CHILLED MELON AND GINGER SOUP

Hot sun, little crackling sounds among the wheat, increasing as the wind blew.
Richard Jefferies, *Diaries* 1884

A very refreshing soup for an *al fresco* lunch or supper in the garden. Ideal, also, to take on a picnic if a flask is filled with ice-cubes and the soup poured over. It will be refreshingly cold when required, especially if the day is as hot as described by Richard Jefferies on 22 July 1884.

Serves 6–8, depending on appetites

2 small well flavoured melons
6 pieces of preserved ginger in syrup
¼ litre/½ pint [1¼ cups] single [light] cream
¼ litre/½ pint [1¼ cups] natural Greek yoghurt
2 tbsp sugar
chopped mint

Cut the melons in half and remove the pips. Spoon the flesh into a bowl. Slice the ginger and add to the melon. Mix in the sugar and yoghurt.

Put the mixture into a liquidiser and blend until very smooth, then empty into a bowl. Blend in the cream.

Put to chill in the refrigerator or pour into a flask which has been chilled and has a few ice cubes added.

When ready to serve, sprinkle the top with chopped mint and a swirl of double [heavy] cream.

CHILLED CUCUMBER AND LOVAGE SOUP

Once popular in the old herb gardens, lovage is today not so well known, but it is well worth growing for its unique aromatic celery flavour that it imparts to soups, stews and salads.

The Highlanders of Scotland used to eat the leaves first thing in the morning to preserve them from colds. It was also chewed as a substitute for tobacco.

This chilled soup is delicious for a dinner party or easily made and transported to any sporting occasion for a picnic.

To serve 4–6

1 medium sized onion, peeled and finely chopped
1 small clove garlic, crushed with a little salt
2 small or 1 large cucumber, peeled and chopped
2 large sprigs fresh lovage, washed and chopped
125 g/4 oz carton natural yoghurt
¾ litre/1½ pints [3¾ cups] chicken or vegetable stock
salt and white pepper

Put all the ingredients into one bowl and mix well together.

Liquidise one third of the ingredients at a time until smooth and creamy. (If a jellied stock has been used, the soup may need to be slackened with a little water to correct the consistency.) Pour into chilled soup bowls and decorate with a sprig of lovage and slice of cucumber.

If for a picnic, pour into a chilled flask.

An Elegant Lady on a Grey
by Alfred de Dreux.

The Tennis Party, 1891,
by Edward Frederick Brewtnall.

CHILLED CURRIED APPLE SOUP

To serve 4–6

After Goodwood came Cowes Week, and
Cowes Roads were filled to overflowing
with every description of craft. It was a
glorious sight to see the big racing yachts
come swooping down the Solent with
every stitch of canvas set. My mother and
I often stayed at Eaglehurst with Count
and Countess Batthyany. They lived in
foreign style; we lunched and dined at
small tables in the garden which in the
evening was lit up by Chinese lanterns.
The view of the sea and the twinkling
lights from the yachts made a lovely
picture in the moonlight.

Chit-Chat, Lady Augusta Fane, *c.* 1884

What a perfect setting for a lunch or
dinner party. This soup is ideal for such
an occasion as a summer first course, or
for taking on picnics. The use of fresh
coconut milk, although optional, does
impart a delicious underlying flavour to
the soup and complements the curry paste.

3 tbsp vegetable oil
2 medium sized onions, peeled and finely
  chopped
3 tsp curry paste
¾ litre/1½ pints [3¾ cups] chicken stock
1 kg/2 lb eating apples, peeled, cored and
  sliced
juice of 1 small lemon
¼ litre /½ pint [1¼ cups] coconut milk
  (optional)
125 ml/¼ pint [½ cup] natural Greek
  yoghurt
2 tsp mango chutney
1 clove garlic, crushed with a little salt
salt and black pepper

Heat the oil in a large pan, add the onion,
garlic and chopped apple, cover and
sweat, stirring from time to time to
prevent sticking. When the apple and
onion are soft, add the curry paste, lemon
juice and the stock. Simmer for 20 minutes
until all the ingredients are well blended.

Add the chutney, mix well and remove
from the heat. Allow the liquid to cool
then liquidise until smooth. Whisk in the
yoghurt and coconut milk.

Chill overnight if possible. Serve with
a swirl of cream on top.

The seasonings can be added at any
time, but care must be taken not to
overpower the subtle flavour of the soup.

DEVILLED WHITEBAIT

Multitudes of these tiny sprat and herring are to be found in the River Thames during May to August. For many years, Parliament used to have a 'Whitebait Dinner' before the close of the session.

Household Management,
Mrs Beeton, 1861

To serve 4

500 g/1 lb whitebait, fresh or frozen
2 tsp salt
125 g/4 oz [1 cup] flour
300 ml/½ pint [1¼ cups] milk
1 tsp black pepper
1 tsp cayenne pepper
lemon slices
a few parsley sprigs

Defrost the whitebait if frozen. Put the fish into the milk for about 5 minutes (this helps the flour to stick). Drain the whitebait using a fine sieve.

Put the salt, flour and peppers into a plastic or polythene bag.

Heat a pan of oil, about half full, or use a deep fat fryer.

Shake the whitebait in the bag of flour and pepper until well coated all over.

When the oil is hot, fry the whitebait, a few at a time for about 2 minutes, until they are brown and crisp.

Remove the fish onto a baking tray spread with absorbent kitchen paper. Keep them warm while frying the remainder of the fish.

When all are cooked and drained of fat, put them onto four warm plates and sprinkle over a little more cayenne pepper, and garnish with the lemon slices and parsley. Serve with brown bread and butter, or toast and butter.

SOLE FILLETS WITH A FRESH ORANGE MAYONNAISE

Come when the leaf comes, angle with me,
Come when the bee hums, crossing
the lea;
Come with the wild flowers,
Come with the mild showers,
Come when the singing bird calleth
for thee.
An Angler's Invitation,
Thomas Tod Stoddart (1810–1880)

A refreshing and tasty first course, this dish is served cold with a mixed green salad, making it ideal for a summer lunch or picnic. Naturally, by increasing the quantity, it can also be served as a main dish. Fresh fish is recommended for best results.

To serve 4

4 large lemon sole fillets, skin removed
juice of 1 small lemon
2 tbsp medium white wine
30 g/1 oz [2 tbsp] butter
sprig of fresh tarragon
salt and white pepper
For the orange mayonnaise
125 ml/¼ pint [½ cup] good mayonnaise
4 oranges, peeled, pith removed and
segmented
grated rind [zest] of 1 orange
2 tsp white wine vinegar
1 tsp caster [superfine] sugar

Pre-heat the oven 180°C/350°F/Gas
Mark 4

Line an oven-proof dish with foil. Roll up
the sole fillets and lay them on the foil in
the dish. Season well, pour in the wine and
lemon juice, dot the fish with the butter,
put in the sprig of tarragon and seal the
foil well to form a tight 'parcel'. Cook in
the pre-heated oven for 20 minutes.

When cooked, remove the fish from
the oven and allow to cool. Do not
refrigerate or the flesh will become too
firm.

To prepare the mayonnaise: put the
made mayonnaise into a bowl, add the
grated rind [zest] of the orange, wine
vinegar, and the sugar. Blend thoroughly
together.

When the fish has cooled, lay it on a
bed of lettuce on a serving dish and coat
with the orange mayonnaise. Decorate
with the prepared orange segments and
sprigs of fresh parsley.

The juice from the oranges is not used
for the mayonnaise, as this would make
the consistancy far too runny. The grated
rind [zest] is sufficient to give a delicate
orange flavour, and this also will not mask
the flavour of the sole.

SCOTTISH KIPPER MOUSSE

When the day is far spent and tracks are
made for home, turning out of the wood
you come upon all the glory of the yellow
moon, just rising over the eastern hill, and
glittering in the waters of the loch; the
horses quicken their pace, lights twinkle in
the distance, and now as you swing in at
the gate of the lodge grounds a savoury
whiff courts your nostrils from the shining
kitchen window, while as you turn the
corner to the door the first skirl of the
pipes warns you that it is already half-past
eight, the ladies are waiting, and you must
be quick down to dinner.

Going to the Moors,
Ronald Eden, 1979

The best kippers are from Northumberland, the Isle of Man, East Anglia, and of
course Loch Fyne; these are now sadly in
short supply due to the decline in the
herring fishing industry. There are,
however, the readily available 'ginger-
dyed' variety found in supermarkets and
fishmongers. This mousse is an excellent
dish for a first course when giving a
luncheon or dinner party after a day's
sport.

To serve 8

½ kg/1 lb boneless kipper fillets
¼ litre /½ pint [1¼ cups] milk
30 g/1 oz [2 tbsp] unsalted butter
30 g/1 oz [2 tbsp] plain [all purpose] flour
125 ml/¼ pint [½ cup] crème fraîche
2 large eggs, separated
juice of 1 small lemon
½ tsp ground mace
15 g/½ oz powdered gelatine [unflavoured
   gelatin] dissolved in 3 tbsp water

Put the milk into a pan and poach the
kipper fillets until cooked (about 5
minutes). Drain off the milk and reserve.
Remove any dark skin from the fillets.

Melt the butter in the pan and stir in
the flour, cook gently until it turns to a
light beige colour.

Remove from the heat and add the

poaching milk a little at a time, stirring well until the mixture is smooth.

Return to the heat and bring to the boil, stirring in the mace and lemon juice.

Remove from the heat once more and beat in the egg yolks, add the dissolved gelatine and mix well. Allow to cool.

When cool, liquidise the sauce and the kipper fillets together. Fold in the crème fraîche (mayonnaise can be substituted if a richer mousse is required).

Whisk the egg whites until firm then fold into the mousse. Pour into a large dish or individual dishes or pots. Allow to set in a cool place (if guests are unpunctual, this mousse will stand ready without spoiling).

Serve with a twist of lemon and wholemeal bread or toast.

DOUBLE SALMON MOUSSE

This mousse is very versatile, in that it can be easily transported for a picnic, being put into a bowl and then turned out when required; or it can be put into small individual 'moulds', turned out, and served as a first course for a lunch or dinner party. A ham or chicken mousse can be made in the same way, by lining a bowl with very thinly sliced ham, and putting the ham or chicken mousse into the bowl, thereby making a double ham or chicken mousse.

To serve 4

4 slices of smoked salmon
180 g/6 oz fresh salmon, poached (retain liquid)
juice of $\frac{1}{2}$ lemon
90 g/3 oz [$\frac{1}{2}$ cup] double [heavy] cream

cayenne pepper to taste
30 g/1 oz [2 tbsp] unsalted butter
30 g/1 oz [2 tbsp] plain [all purpose] flour
150 ml/$\frac{1}{4}$ pint [$\frac{1}{2}$ cup] fish stock, reserved from the salmon poaching liquid*
a pinch of salt
4 teacups or ramekins for the mousse

Line the sides and bottoms of the teacups or ramekins with the smoked salmon. Put to one side.

Melt the butter in a saucepan, add the flour, and cook gently for about 2 minutes. Gradually pour in the stock and blend well together.

Pound the cooked salmon and add it to the sauce mixture in the pan, season with the salt and cayenne pepper, blend in the lemon juice. Put to one side and allow to cool.

When cold, lightly whip the cream, and fold into the fish mixture, making sure the cream is thoroughly blended in. Spoon the mousse into the prepared cups, cover, and allow to set.

If the mousse is to be taken on a picnic, and if desired, cut four circles of brown bread to the size of the cup, butter on one side and place on top of the mousse; when the mousse is turned out it will be sitting on a brown bread base.

When the mousse is required, take a sharp knife and run the blade around the edge of the mousse to loosen it. This can be done at home, and the mousses wrapped in clingfilm for transporting.

*If the liquid from the poached salmon was not retained, take 3 tsp of gelatine softened in 3 tbsp of cold water and added to the hot sauce before folding in the whipped cream.

STEAK TARTARE

Terry Biddlecombe's variation of this marvellous dish is very simple to make and requires no cooking. Terry recommends that it should be followed by three large glasses of port, vintage or non-vintage depending on who is paying the bill.

To serve 2

300 g/10 oz fillet steak, finely chopped
1 small onion, peeled and grated
2 cloves of garlic, crushed with a little salt
½ tsp capers
2 tsp gherkins, finely chopped
dash of tabasco sauce
2 tsp Worcester sauce
salt and black pepper to taste
1 egg yolk
2 good tbsp brandy

Put all the ingredients into a large bowl and mix well. Shape into a circle and place onto a plate. Serve with a mixed salad and French dressing.

CURRIED BEEF RISSOLES WITH MUSTARD SAUCE

The rissoles were then candidates for his custom. 'Large marbles', observed Mr Jorrocks aloud to himself – 'large marbles', repeated he, as he at length succeeded in penetrating the hide of one with a spoon. 'Might as well eat lead', observed he aloud, sending them away too.

Handley Cross,
R. S. Surtees, 1843

Unlike the ones given to poor Mr Jorrocks, these rissoles are delicious served as a first course or as a main dish for a shooting lunch or supper, or on any day spent in the country. Plain boiled rice is a good accompaniment to the rissoles.

To serve 4 as a main dish

For the rissoles
¼ kg/8 oz minced beef, cooked
60 g/2 oz [good ½ cup] brown
    breadcrumbs
1 egg, beaten
1 onion, peeled and finely chopped
2 tsp curry paste
2 tsp tomato pureé [paste]
1 small clove garlic, crushed with a little
    salt
2 tsp oil
lots of ground black pepper
For the mustard sauce
45 g/1½ oz [3 tbsp] butter
45 g/1½ oz [scant ½ cup] plain [all purpose]
    flour
425 ml/¾ pint [2 cups] brown stock or 1
    small tin condensed consommé, made

up with water to the required
    measurement
4 tsp English mustard
150 ml/¼ pint [½ cup] single [light] cream
2 level tsp caster [superfine] sugar
salt and ground black pepper

To make the rissoles, sauté the chopped onion in the oil until soft. Put all the ingredients into a bowl and mix well.

Form the mixture into even-sized balls or 'cakes' and sauté in hot oil until a nice brown colour.

To make the sauce, melt the butter in a pan, add the flour and cook for a couple of minutes until a roux is formed and is a light biscuit colour.

Add the stock or consommé a little at a time, stirring well. Add the sugar, salt and pepper, mix well, then add the mustard. Pour in the cream and check the seasoning. Blend the ingredients thoroughly together until they become a smooth creamy sauce.

Serve in a warm sauce boat or pour over the rissoles. Sprinkle with chopped parsley to decorate.

SPICED PORK AND APPLE PASTIES

Goodwood is perfect when the weather is fine, a real racing picnic.

Chit-Chat,
Lady Augusta Fane, *c.* 1884

These spiced pasties are ideal for taking on a picnic. They are easily prepared using any left over cold pork and are delicious hot or cold.

For 4 pasties

1 large cooking apple, peeled, cored and
    sliced
1 large potato, peeled and sliced
1 medium onion, peeled and finely
    chopped
500 g/1lb shortcrust [pie] pastry
125 g/4 oz carrot, peeled and diced
350 g/12 oz pork, minced (cooked or
    uncooked, depending on whether the
    pork is left over or bought)
1 sage leaf
1 egg beaten for glaze
cayenne pepper to taste
1 tbsp chopped parsley
salt and white pepper

Prepare the pastry and allow it to rest.

Mix together in a large bowl the diced
apple, potato, carrot and onion. Add the
minced pork and herbs. Season very well
with the cayenne and white pepper and
the salt. Mix in thoroughly.

Cut 4 large circles of pastry (a medium
sized plate is an ideal measure). Pile the
pork mixture evenly between each circle
of pastry. Moisten one half of the pastry
with the beaten egg, fold the pastry over
and press the edges firmly together.

Brush each pasty well with the
remaining beaten egg. Make a couple of
holes in each pasty to let out the steam.

Bake in the oven at 220°C/425°F/Gas
Mark 7 for ten minutes, then lower the
temperature to 175°C/350°F/Gas Mark 4,
and cook for a further 30 to 35 minutes.

This cooking time is correct if the
vegetables have been finely sliced and
diced, but if the pieces have been cut more
roughly, then the cooking time has to be
increased to compensate.

ROLLED BREAST OF VEAL WITH HERB STUFFING AND A CELERY SAUCE

A very veal dinner – at a dinner given by
Lord Polkemmet, a Scotch nobleman and
judge, his guests saw, when the covers
were removed, that the fare consisted of
veal broth, a roasted fillet of veal, veal
cutlets, a veal pie, a calf's head, and calf's
foot jelly. The judge observing the surprise
of his guests, volunteered an explanation
'Ou, ay, it's a cauf; when we kill a beast,
we just eat up ae side, and doun the tither.

Household Management,
Mrs Beeton, 1861

A breast of lamb can also be used for this
recipe, but it is a lot more fatty.

To serve 4–6

a breast of veal (about 1½ kg/3 lb)
60 g/2 oz [4 tbsp] fresh mixed herbs,
    chopped finely
grated rind [zest] of 1 lemon
a little grated nutmeg
a little grated mace
125 g/4 oz [1¼ cups] white breadcrumbs
2 tbsp dripping [beef fat]
60 g/2 oz [¼ cup] unsalted butter
flour for dredging
salt and black pepper
For the celery sauce
1 head celery, cleaned and chopped
60 g/2 oz [¼ cup] unsalted butter
a little fresh parsley and thyme, chopped
1 medium onion, peeled and chopped
salt and black pepper
150 ml/¼ pint [½ cup] single [light] cream
300 ml/½ pint [1¼ cup] veal or lamb stock

Bone the veal without cutting through the breast (your butcher will do this for you but ask for the bones as these are for the stock). Lay the meat flat and sprinkle the inside with the mace, fresh herbs, grated lemon peel, breadcrumbs, nutmeg, salt and pepper. Roll up tightly and secure with skewers. With the dripping, grease a sheet of kitchen foil and wrap the veal securely inside.

Roast for 1 to 1½ hours at 170°C/ 325°F/Gas Mark 3. Twenty minutes before the end of cooking time, remove the foil, baste with the butter, dredge with the flour and allow the joint to brown.

To make the sauce put the butter into a pan and fry the chopped onion and celery until tender. Add the herbs and seasonings. Pour in the stock and simmer for 15 minutes until the celery and onion are really cooked. Add any meat juices from the roasting pan after removing any fat.

Put the sauce into a blender and liquidise until smooth. Sieve the pureé into a large saucepan,* check the seasonings and stir in the cream. Heat gently but do not boil.

*If the celery is very young and not at all stringy, it is not necessary to sieve the pureé. Serve separately.

MINCED CHICKEN CHAUDFROID

This is an adaptation to the original recipe which uses whole chicken breasts, but by mincing the meat, it can easily be eaten with a fork for buffets or picnics.

To serve 4

salt and white pepper
4 chicken breasts
4 tbsp medium white wine
3 slices of onion
1 small carrot cut into julien strips
150 ml/¼ pint [½ cup] double [heavy] cream
3 tsp gelatine [unflavoured gelatin] or aspic dissolved in 4 tbsp water
30 g/1 oz [2 tbsp] butter
5 sprigs fresh tarragon

Place the chicken breasts in an oven-proof dish, putting a sprig of tarragon under the chicken. Pour over the wine, add the onion and carrot slices, dot with the butter, season well with white pepper and salt. Cover, and cook for 35 minutes or until tender at 160°C/325°F/Gas Mark 3–3½.

Remove the chicken from the liquid and strain the juices; discard the vegetables but reserve the liquid. Add the dissolved gelatine or aspic to the chicken liquid, mix thoroughly. Pour in the cream and stir. Put the mixture into a liquidizer along with a sprig of tarragon and blend well. The sauce should be smooth and creamy.

When the cooked chicken breasts have cooled, mince finely, adding a little of the sauce to bind the meat. Form the meat either back into the shape of a chicken breast, or into any shape that you desire.

Allow the sauce to cool, then with the moulded chicken meat shapes on a wire rack, pour over the almost setting sauce. It will probably take about two coats to cover properly.

Lay a sprig of tarragon on top of each chicken shape and serve with a fresh green salad and/or new potatoes.

CHICKEN PATTIES

The breezy call of incense-breathing
                morn,
The swallow twitt'ring from the
              straw-built shed,
The cock's shrill clarion, or the
              echoing horn,
No more shall rouse them from the
              lowly bed.
Elegy written in a country churchyard,
Thomas Grey (1716–1771)

These chicken patties are very simple to make. They can be made in advance, and stored in the refrigerator until required. Turkey can be used as an alternative to chicken.

To make about 12–16 small patties

1 kg/2 lb chicken, cooked and minced
1 large onion, peeled and sliced
1 tsp chopped parsley
$\frac{1}{2}$ tsp chopped tarragon
$\frac{1}{2}$ tsp ground nutmeg
125 g/4 oz [$1\frac{1}{3}$ cups] white breadcrumbs
1 small clove garlic, crushed with a little
    salt
salt and black pepper
3 eggs, beaten

Combine all the ingredients well together, bind with the beaten egg. Form the mixture into round, flat cakes. Chill well in the refrigerator.

When required, fry in hot fat for about 7 minutes on each side, until golden brown.

Serve with creamed or sautéed potatoes and any fresh green vegetable or salad.

POULET CHANTILLY
(A chilled chicken salad)

Leathery breeches, spreading stables,
  Shining saddles left behind –
To the down the string of horses
  Moving out of sight and mind.
  Upper Lambourn, John Betjeman, 1906

This is an excellent summer party dish,
ideal for Ascot or any outdoor occasion.
It is best made the day before as it
improves with chilling and keeping in the
refrigerator. Chantilly is derived from the
French, meaning lace, which is a very
good description of this unusual and
delicious salad.

To serve 4–5

1 medium sized cooked chicken
125 g/4 oz mushrooms, cleaned and
    quartered
250 g/8 oz [1 cup] rice
juice of $\frac{1}{2}$ lemon
30 g/1 oz [2 tbsp] unsalted butter
$\frac{1}{4}$ litre /$\frac{1}{2}$ pint [1$\frac{1}{4}$ cups] mayonnaise
    (home-made)
8 small onions, peeled
1 tomato, peeled and quartered
1 red pepper
1 green pepper
150 ml/$\frac{1}{4}$ pint [$\frac{1}{2}$ cup] olive oil
150 ml/$\frac{1}{4}$ pint [$\frac{1}{2}$ cup] dry white wine
300 ml/$\frac{1}{2}$ pint [1$\frac{1}{4}$ cups] double [heavy]
    cream
300 ml/$\frac{1}{2}$ pint [1$\frac{1}{4}$ cups] vegetable or
    chicken stock
1 bay leaf
salt and pepper
a little extra stock

1 heart of lettuce and 1 hardboiled egg to
    garnish

Cut the peppers in half and remove the
pith and seeds. Cut into small strips and
place them in a pan of cold water, bring
to the boil and boil for 5 minutes.
Remove, and drain, put to one side.

Put the wine, oil, lemon juice and
stock into a large pan. Add the
mushrooms, onions, tomato, bay leaf and
seasonings. Boil for 7 to 10 minutes, until
the onions are soft. Strain off the liquid
and make up with the extra stock to
600 ml/1$\frac{1}{4}$ pints [3 cups].

Melt the butter in a large pan, add the
rice. Stir over a low heat until the rice is
opaque, then remove from the heat and
add the stock, onions, mushrooms and
tomato, season well. Cover with
greaseproof [wax] paper and a lid. Cook
in a moderate oven 190°C/375°F/Gas
Mark 5, for 25 to 30 minutes. When the
rice is tender, remove from the oven and
spread it out on a large plate to cool.

Remove any skin from the chicken and
cut the meat into small strips. Whip the
cream until fairly stiff and fold in the
mayonnaise gently.

Heap the rice mixture onto a serving
dish and make a well in the centre. Fold
the chicken strips into the mayonnaise and
cream, then pour over the rice, with the
main bulk in the centre of the well.

Around the edge of the well, arrange
the lettuce leaves. Sieve the yolk of the
hard boiled egg, and sprinkle over the top
of the rice. The chopped whites can be
arranged around the outside edge. A little
chopped parsley can also be sprinkled
over.

Serve very cold.

RABBIT AND MUSTARD PIE

Devilish good dinner — cold, but capital peeped into the room this morning – fowls and pies, and all that sort of thing – pleasant these fellows – well behaved too, very.

> Dingley Dell and Muggleton Cricket Dinner, at the Blue Lion Inn, Muggleton
> from
> *Pickwick Papers*, Charles Dickens, 1837

We rather think that Mr Pickwick would have approved of this rabbit pie, especially as it is hot and not cold as mentioned at the cricket dinner. It can be prepared the day before you require it, so it is a great time-saver as well as a delicious dish.

To serve 6

1 prepared rabbit, jointed, tossed in seasoned flour
180 g/6 oz smoked streaky bacon, rind removed
1 leek, trimmed and washed
1 clove garlic, crushed with a little salt
4 tsp Dijon mustard
150 ml/¼ pint [½ cup] double [heavy] cream
1 bay leaf
2 tsp chopped parsley
1 large carrot, peeled and thinly sliced
2 tbsp vegetable oil
60 g/2 oz [½ stick] unsalted butter
150 ml/¼ pint [½ cup] stock
150 ml/¼ pint [½ cup] dry white wine
1 onion, peeled and finely chopped
salt and black pepper
¼ kg/8 oz shortcrust [pie], flaky or puff pastry for the lid

In a large pan, melt the oil and butter together. Add the rabbit joints, cook until just brown to seal in the juices. Remove and put into a casserole dish.

Chop the bacon and fry this for a couple of minutes in the pan, remove and add to the casserole.

Put the chopped onion, carrot, leek, and crushed garlic into the pan, put on a lid, and cook until soft. When ready, add the vegetables to the rabbit.

Pour the stock and wine over the rabbit meat, add the bay leaf, season well, and cook slowly for 2¾ hours at oven temperature 160°C/325°F/Gas Mark 3. The rabbit meat should be very tender when cooked.

When the casserole is cooked thoroughly remove meat from joints if desired. Pour the casserole liquid into a pan along with the mustard, and simmer. Stir well to blend in the mustard.

Remove the pan from the heat, pour in the cream, sprinkle in the chopped parsley. Remove the bay leaf from the casserole and put the rabbit and vegetables into the mustard sauce. Allow to cool. When the meat and sauce is cold, put into a pie dish and cover with the pastry lid. Brush the pastry with milk or beaten egg and put into a very hot oven – 220°/C425°F/Gas Mark 7 – and cook for around 20 minutes; reduce the temperature after that time to 175°C/350°F/Gas Mark 4, and cook for a further 30 minutes. If necessary, cover the pastry lid with foil to prevent over browning.

When ready, wrap the dish in a white napkin, and serve with fresh vegetables and creamed potatoes.

VENISON STEAKS WITH A CLARET AND DAMSON SAUCE

Dined in Hall at the High Table upon a neck of venison and breast made into pasty, a ham, fowls and two pies. It is a venison feast which we have once a year about this time. Two bucks one year, and 1 buck another year is always sent from Whaddon Chase and divided between the wardens, the senior fellows and us.

The Diary of a Country Parson,
James Woodforde,
17 August 1763

To serve 4

4 venison steaks
60 g/2 oz [¼ cup] unsalted butter
2 tbsp damson jelly
large wine glass good claret
2 tbsp jellied stock
salt and coarsley ground black pepper

Melt the butter in a heavy based pan and fry the steaks according to taste, taking care not to over-cook or they will be very dry. When cooked, remove the steaks and keep them warm.

Deglaze the pan with the claret and mix well with the meat juices that are in the pan. Add the damson jelly, jellied stock and the seasonings. Cook until reduced to a syrupy sauce, stirring all the time.

Put the venison onto a hot serving dish and pour over the sauce. Serve with creamed potatoes, runner beans, and/or carrots.

A large chunk of home-made bread would mop up the sauce very well, if appetites permit.

PIGEON PIE
(Epsom Grandstand Recipe)

According to the Reverend John A. Clark in 1840, Derby Day seemed to have the qualities of a huge picnic, a mammoth country fair, and a dangerous public riot! During the intervals between the races, the ground was filled with jugglers, gamesters, rope-dancers, fortune tellers, rows of gambling booths splendidly hung with crimson and beautiful tapestry.

There was one Derby Day though, that put a stop to the gaming, gambling and the picnics; the morning of 22 May 1867. Henry Blyth tells us in *The Pocket Venus*, 1966, 'The day dawned grey and bitterly cold. As the day wore on, biting winds, sleet and finally flurries of snow swept across Epsom Downs. The huge crowds which normally flocked to the course from London were reduced to a trickle', and *The Times*, in its subsequent report of the scene, referred to the inclement weather 'which froze the general current gaiety of the holiday makers. There was a forest of umbrellas on the course and in the stands, and the racegoers slapped their hands for warmth as they watched the horses parading in the paddock.'

How they would have needed a bowl of our Hunter's Soup and a slice of pigeon pie to ward off the bitter weather.

In the original recipe, whole pigeons are used, but for our purpose and present day requirements, pigeon breasts, which can be bought from most good supermarkets and game dealers, are much more convenient.

To serve 5–6

6 pigeon breasts
¾ kg/1½ lb rump [tenderloin] steak, cut
    into pieces about 8 cm/3 in. square
6 slices of ham
6 small knobs butter
4 egg yolks
stock, sufficient to half fill the pie dish
puff pastry, sufficient for the top of the pie
salt and black pepper
a little seasoned flour, for tossing the meat
    before frying
1 tsp fresh tarragon, chopped

Toss the pigeon breasts and pieces of steak
in the seasoned flour.

Melt a little oil in a frying pan, and put
in the pieces of steak, not too much at a
time, or they will not brown. When brown
remove from the pan and put into the
bottom of the pie dish.

Brown the pigeon breasts in the same
way to seal in the juices, remove from the
pan onto a board. Place a knob of butter
on each breast and roll up with a slice of
ham around each. Lay them on the steak.

Season well with salt and pepper. Add
the whole yolks of egg one at a time, half
fill the dish with the stock and sprinkle
over the chopped tarragon.

Roll out the puff pastry, cut a long,
thin strip of pastry and place it around the
edge of the pie dish, dampen with a little
water or milk. Cover the top of the pie
with the remainder of the pastry.

Brush the top with a little milk and
bake in a hot oven 200°C/400°F/Gas Mark
6, for 15 to 20 minutes to brown the
pastry, then lower the heat to 150°C/
300°F/Gas Mark 2 for 2 hours until the
meat is cooked thoroughly. A lid of
kitchen foil over the top of the pie crust
will prevent it browning too much.

COUNTRY FISH PIE

But the fly fisherman seeks the spot because the water is swift at the angle of the stream and broken by a ledge of rock. He can throw up stream – the line falls soft as silk on the slow eddy below the rock, and the fly is drawn gently towards him across the current. When a natural fly approaches the surface of running water, and flutters along just above it, it encounters a light air, which flows in the same direction as the stream. Facing this surface breeze, the fly cannot progress straight up the river, but is carried sideways across it. This motion the artificial fly imitates; a trout takes it, and is landed on the stones.

The Life of the Fields,
Richard Jefferies, 1884

Almost any fish of your choice is good for this recipe. It can be sea or river fish, it is really a matter of preference, taste and availability.

To serve 4

$\frac{1}{2}$ kg/1 lb fresh fish: trout, cod, haddock etc.
3 slices of lean ham
small pinch of cayenne pepper
3 hard boiled eggs
salt and black pepper
1 tsp anchovy essence [extract]
1 tsp tomato pureé [paste]
45 g/1$\frac{1}{2}$ oz [3 tbsp] unsalted butter
45 g/1$\frac{1}{2}$ oz [3 tbsp] plain [all purpose] flour
a little chopped fresh basil or parsley, or mixture of both
$\frac{1}{4}$ kg/8 oz shortcrust [pie] pastry
$\frac{1}{4}$ litre /$\frac{1}{2}$ pint [1$\frac{1}{4}$ cups] milk

Into a saucepan put the fish and milk, season with the salt and black pepper and gently cook until the fish is tender. Remove the fish from the pan and reserve the poaching liquid. Flake the fish, discarding any skin and bones.

Remove the egg shells and discard. Slice the egg into rings. Cut the ham into small strips. Put the fish, eggs and ham in layers in an oven-proof pie dish. Sprinkle over the cayenne pepper and season with the salt and black pepper.

Melt the butter in a saucepan and add the flour. Cook for about 2 to 3 minutes, stirring well. Take the reserved fish liquid and slowly pour it into the saucepan. Mix well together until you have a smooth sauce consistency. Add the tomato pureé [paste], anchovy essence [extract] and chopped herbs.

Pour the sauce over the fish and ham (if there is any sauce left over, reserve it for serving in a separate bowl). Cover with the pastry. Brush over with a little milk or beaten egg and bake in the oven at 200°C/400°F/Gas Mark 6 for about 20 to 25 minutes until the pastry is brown and golden.

RIVER TROUT WITH MELTED BUTTER

I wind about, and in and out,
With here a blossom sailing,
And here and there a lusty trout,
And here and there a grayling

from *The Brook*,
Alfred Lord Tennyson

I am indebted to the late Sir Gordon Richards for this recipe; it was a great favourite in his racing days when a light diet was most important. It no doubt helped to a certain extent to keep Sir Gordon in trim to enable him to pass Fred Archer's record in 1943, riding 2,749 winners.

1 trout per person, gutted, cleaned, head
    removed if desired
a little salt
melted, unsalted butter

With a sharp knife make a few shallow slits in the skin of the fish on both sides (this helps to keep their shape). Sprinkle each trout with salt, roll them in the melted butter and grill [broil], turning the fish from time to time and basting with more butter.

Serve the cooked trout on a hot serving dish decorated with sprigs of fresh parsley and slices of lemon. A little more melted butter can be poured over if required.

This recipe is also very good for barbecues: prepare in the same way and cook over charcoal which is glowing hot.

Fresh tarragon can also be served as an accompanying herb, chopped and sprinkled over.

LOBSTER SOUFFLÉ

The chaplain's errand was to inform us, that Mr Thornhill had provided music and refreshments; and intended that night giving the young ladies a ball by moonlight, on the grass plot before our door.

The Vicar of Wakefield
Oliver Goldsmith, 1764

If only summer weather in England was as reliable as in the Vicar of Wakefield's time. It is not very difficult to imagine the Vicar's daughters helping themselves to a lobster soufflé, similar to the one described here.

A very delicate soufflé, ideal for picnics or summer lunch parties, or as a first course for a special dinner party. I think the accompaniment has to be iced champagne, Brut or Rosé.

To serve 6–8

½ kg/1 lb lobster meat; reserve the shell
125 ml/¼ pint [½ cup] whipped cream
salt and white pepper
6 tbsp milk
3 level tsp gelatine [unflavoured gelatin]
3 hard boiled eggs
2 skinned tomatoes
handful of very finely shredded crisp
    lettuce
sufficient mayonnaise to fold in the salad
    ingredients
60 g/2 oz [4 tbsp] unsalted butter

Chop the lobster meat finely then fold it into the whipped cream. Season to taste.

Pound the lobster shell until finely ground, put into a saucepan with the butter and the milk. Simmer over a gentle heat until the flavour of the shell is well infused into the milk. When cold, pour through a sieve into the lobster and cream mixture. Discard the shell.

Dissolve the gelatine in 4 tbsp water, over a saucepan of hot water. When completely dissolved, stir into the lobster and cream mixture.

Chop the hard boiled eggs, cut up the skinned tomatoes and mix with the shredded lettuce. Fold in the mayonnaise, a spoon at a time so as not to overdo the quantity.

Put these salad ingredients into the base of a soufflé dish: it should reach about half way up the dish. Pour on the lobster and cream soufflé mixture and allow to set.

If desired a thin layer of aspic jelly slightly coloured with pink cochineal can be put over the top of the set soufflé, but this is entirely a matter of preference.

Serve well chilled with brown bread and butter.

COLD POACHED LOBSTER WITH VERTÉ SAUCE

We're off to the races,
With smiles on our faces,
Lobster salad, and champagne, and chat;
Prime Newcastle salmon,
And Westphalia 'gammon';
But there's no mistake about that.
The Derby, 'Craven', 1840

1 lobster per person, or between two, depending on appetites

Bring to the boil a very large saucepan of water. Put the lobster into the rapidly boiling water and cook for ten to twenty minutes. Allow to cool, and cut the lobster in half lengthways.

Verté sauce: to make enough for 4 servings

300 ml/½ pint [1¼ cup] mayonnaise
1 handful spinach leaves, chopped and washed
1 tbsp lovage, chopped
2 tbsp parsley, chopped
1 tbsp tarragon, chopped
salt and black pepper

Blanch the herbs and spinach leaves in boiling, salted water. Drain well and put them into a liquidiser. Pour the mayonnaise onto the herbs and spinach and blend well together until smooth. Season to taste, pour into a bowl or over the cold lobster.

The Hunting Luncheon
by J-B. Oudry.

Pheasants on the Moor, 1860,
by John Christopher Bell.

PEPPERED GINGER SALMON

A birr; a whirr; a salmon's on,
A goodly fish; a thumper;
Bring up, bring up the ready gaff,
And if we land him we shall quaff
Another glorious bumper:
Hark; tis the music of the reel,
The strong, the quick, the steady;
The line darts from the active wheel,
Have all things right and ready

The Taking of the Salmon,
Thomas Tod-Stoddart (1810–1880)

To serve 4

4 fresh salmon steaks, skin removed
125 g/4 oz [½ cup] unsalted butter
4 tsp roughly crushed peppercorns
6 whole pieces preserved ginger, thinly
    sliced
1 sherry glass dry vermouth
juice of ½ lemon
2 tbsp brandy
300 g/½ pint [1¼ cups] double [heavy] or
    single [light] cream

Press the crushed peppercorns onto each
side of the salmon. Melt the butter in a
heavy-based frying pan. Cook the salmon
in the butter for 4 minutes on each side.
Remove from the pan and keep warm.

Pour the vermouth and brandy into
the residue of butter in the pan and cook
until reduced by half the quantity. Add the
lemon juice and ginger, stir well then pour
in the cream. Simmer gently until the
consistency is smooth and creamy (a little
water may be added to the sauce if it
becomes too thick). Check the seasonings.

Return the salmon to the pan, turn
them in the sauce and cook for 6 minutes.

Serve immediately with the sauce
poured over. Sprinkle over a little chopped
chives or dill.

ANCHOVY TOAST

A very easy dish to prepare, ideal for
breakfast, a light lunch or supper dish, or
as a savoury after a dinner party. The
anchovy paste, as made here, bears little
resemblance to the bought paste: it is
much creamier and tastier. It also keeps
for about two weeks in the refrigerator, or
it can be frozen until required.

To serve 4–6

4 tins anchovies, drained
4 tbsp milk
¼ kg/8 oz [1 cup] unsalted butter
8 tsp thick cream
freshly ground black pepper

Soak the drained anchovies in the milk for
3–4 minutes to remove some of the salt.
Drain off the milk. Put the anchovies into
a liquidiser and blend to a paste. Add the
thick cream and blend once more. Blend
in the butter, a little at a time. Season well
with the black pepper.

Put the paste into an earthenware pot
and cover. When required, spread upon
thick slices of hot toast.

HOT CHEESE SOUFFLÉ
WITH MUSTARD

When this soufflé is cooking, resist the temptation to look before cooking time is up; if you do, your soufflé may collapse. Any strong-tasting cheese such as Gruyère, Parmesan or a mature Cheddar is good for this dish.

To serve 4–6

4 tbsp grated strong flavoured cheese
cayenne pepper
45 g/1½ oz [3 tbsp] unsalted butter
1 tsp made mustard
300 ml/½ pint [1 cup] milk
1 tsp plain [all purpose] flour
4 egg yolks
5 egg whites
2 tbsp brown breadcrumbs
salt to taste

Grease a 18 cm/7 in. soufflé dish and a strip of greaseproof [waxed] paper with a little butter. The greaseproof paper should be of double thickness and cut about 18 cm/7 in. wide and long enough to overlap about 8 cm/3 in. round the outside of the dish, making a 5 cm/2 in. fold along one side. Shake the breadcrumbs around the inside of the greased dish. Butter the strip above the fold, wrap the paper around the dish with the fold at the base and turned inwards. The greased section should stand a good 8 cm/3 in. above the dish. Secure the paper with string tied around the dish, and put onto a baking tray. Pre-heat the oven to 375°F/190°C/Gas Mark 5.

   Make a roux in a medium-sized saucepan by melting the butter, then remove from the heat and stir in the flour, season, then blend in the milk. Put back onto the heat and cook until boiling, stirring all the time, draw to one side.

   Add the mustard to the roux and beat in 3 tbsp of the grated cheese. Blend in the egg yolks, one at a time. Whip the egg whites to a firm, snowy mixture, then stir in gently to the cheese mixture. Mix very carefully with a metal spoon, adding the egg white mixture a third at a time. This mixing must be done very gently, or the soufflé may not rise as well as it should.

   Season, then turn the mixture into the dish. Dust the top with the remainder of the grated cheese and any breadcrumbs you may have left. Bake in the top of the oven for 25–30 minutes.

   When ready, the soufflé should be evenly brown and firm to the touch. Serve at once with lots of mustard and plenty of home-made, malted, wholemeal [whole wheat] bread.

FRESH PEACH SALAD WITH A
STILTON AND WALNUT DRESSING

The success of this salad depends upon the ripeness of the peaches. Tinned ones should not be used for this recipe. The Stilton cream blends surprisingly well with the fresh fruity flavour of the peaches.

To serve 4

4 fresh ripe peaches
2 lettuce hearts, halved

For the dressing
125 g/4 oz [½ cup] creamy Stilton cheese
125 g/¼ pint [½ cup] single [light] cream
salt and black pepper
60 g/2 oz [¼ cup] chopped walnuts
a little milk to mix
pinch of cayenne pepper to taste

To make the dressing, break the cheese into small pieces and put into a food blender. Pour in the single [light] cream and blend, adding a little of the milk to prevent the mixture from clogging and becoming too thick.

Season with the peppers and salt, but be careful with the salt as the Stilton may be salty enough for your taste. Put the dressing into a bowl and mix in the chopped walnuts.

Peel and halve the peaches, remove the stones. Turn the peach halves onto a serving plate and spoon over the Stilton dressing. Decorate with the lettuce halves and a sprig of fresh parsley.

FRESH PEAR AND STILTON FLAN

A husband and wife were at a race meeting. 'Pink Nightie' had just come in, in second place, the man knew that his wife had backed it. 'Did you back it both ways?' enquired the husband anxiously. 'No dear, how foolish of me,' she said, 'I didn't realize they were coming back'.
Sporting and Dramatic Yarns,
R. J. B. Sellar, 1925

This flan makes a marvellous 'peace offering' and would soothe many a troubled breast. It also appeases hungry sportsmen. It can be served as a first course, or as a main dish with a fresh salad. Ideal also for picnics as it is as delicious cold as it is hot.

To serve 4

¼ kg/8 oz shortcrust [pie] pastry
1 large onion, peeled and thinly sliced
2 ripe pears
2 large eggs or 3 small
150 ml/¼ pint [½ cup] single [light] cream
90 g/3 oz [scant ¼ cup] Stilton cheese, rind removed
2 tsp chopped (fresh) parsley
60 g/2 oz [4 tbsp] unsalted butter
salt and black pepper

Pre-heat the oven to 190°C/375°F/Gas Mark 5

Line a flan ring with the rolled out pastry, or line a flan dish; if a dish is used, pre-cook the pastry 'blind' as this will prevent the base from becoming soft. Do not over cook, it should not be browned.

Melt the butter in a pan and cook the onion until soft. Allow to cool before lining the bottom of the pastry case with it.

When the onion has cooled, spread onto the pastry base. Peel, core and slice the pears then place them evenly over the onion. Season well.

Put the cream, eggs, parsley and Stilton into a liquidiser and blend together until smooth and creamy. Pour over the pears and onion.

Cook in the pre-heated oven for about 30 minutes until the mixture has set and is golden brown.

ASPARAGUS AND ONION PIE

At Edmonton his loving wife
    From the balcony spied
Her tender husband, wondering much
    To see how he did ride.
'Stop, stop, John Gilpin; – Here's the
                                    house;'
They all at once did cry;
'The dinner waits, and we are tired;'
    Said Gilpin – 'So am I.'

                            John Gilpin,
                William Cowper, 1782

After a ride like that, a pie such as this
would be most welcome and much
needed. It can be eaten cold, but my
preference would be to eat it hot straight
from the oven with small buttered carrots
and well seasoned creamed potatoes.

To serve 6

8 sticks of asparagus
500 g/1 lb shortcrust [pie] pastry
2 potatoes, peeled and thinly sliced
2 medium size onions, peeled and thinly
    chopped
$\frac{1}{4}$ tsp ground mace
150 ml/$\frac{1}{4}$ pint [$\frac{1}{2}$ cup] single [light] cream
2 tsp fresh chopped parsley
salt and white pepper
1 small egg, beaten

Roll out the pastry and with half of it line
a deep pie dish. Prod the base with a fork
and put into a hot oven to seal. Cook for
just long enough for it to be turning light
brown, which prevents the filling from
making the pastry base soggy.

Trim the asparagus and cut into small
even-sized pieces then blanch in boiling
water for a couple of minutes.

When the pie base is ready, put in
alternate layers of potato slices, onion and
asparagus. Mix the cream, parsley, mace,
salt and pepper together, then pour over
the vegetables.

Cover with the remaining pastry,
brush the edges with the beaten egg, crimp
together with the thumb and forefinger.
Brush all over with the egg. Make a couple
of holes in the top, decorate if desired with
pastry leaves and bake in the oven at
200°C/400°F/Gas Mark 6 for 10 to 15
minutes to cook the pastry, then lower the
temperature to 150°C/300°F/Gas Mark 2
and cook for a further 35 minutes.

After that time, test by putting a
skewer through one of the holes in the top
of the pie. If it passes through easily it is
ready, if not, cook for a little while longer.
The cooking time depends upon the
thickness of the slices of vegetables.

BEETROOT AND PORT JELLY

This is a rather unusual way to serve
beetroot. It is an excellent accompaniment
to roast lamb, game birds and venison. If
possible, it is best to use baby beets as the
visual effect is more pleasing, but larger,
older beetroots can be used, sliced or
diced. A good quality port is also essential
for a good flavour to the jelly.

Sufficient to fill a 1 litre/2 pint ring mould
½ kg/1 lb baby beetroots [beets] about
    3 cm/2 in. round
1 tsp salt
180 ml/6 fl oz [¾ cup] good quality port
100 ml/4 fl oz [½ cup] red wine vinegar
1 bay leaf
1 level tbsp gelatine [unflavoured gelatin]
    dissolved in 2 tbsp cold water

Wash the beetroots [beets] and remove
any tops and leaves. Place them into a
large saucepan and cover with sufficient
water to just submerge the vegetables.
Add a little salt and cook until tender.

Drain off the water and reserve
180 ml/6 fl oz [¾ cup] of the liquid. Rub
off the beetroot skin if baby beets are used.

Heat the port in a saucepan, pour in
the red wine vinegar, reserved beetroot
water and add the bay leaf, simmer for 10
minutes. After that time, remove the bay
leaf, and add the well dissolved gelatine.

Allow the mixture to cool but not set.
Place the beetroots around the bottom of
a ring mould then pour in the port liquid.
Chill until set.

When required, dip the mould quickly
into a bowl of boiling water to loosen the
jelly, then turn out onto a large serving
dish. Decorate with sprigs of fresh
watercress.

Individual moulds can also be used,
putting equal amounts of beetroot into
each mould and pouring in the port jelly
mixture as above. Turn out in the same
way as the ring mould.

DEVONSHIRE BRANDY JUNKET

To go 'a-junketing' was once a popular
tea-time treat in the villages along the
Devonshire coast. The top of the junket is
spread with clotted cream and sprinkled
over with cinnamon or nutmeg. A few
rose petals sprinkled over the top also
looks very attractive. As well as being a
pudding in its own right, junket can also
accompany fresh fruit or a fruit pie.

To serve 4–6

1 tbsp brandy, a little more if required
1 tbsp sugar
1 tsp rennet essence
½ litre/1 pint [2½ cups] milk
clotted or double [heavy] cream to serve
a little cinnamon or nutmeg to sprinkle

Pour the milk into a saucepan and bring
to blood heat, do not boil.

Pour the heated milk into a serving
bowl and stir in the brandy and sugar.
Lastly, add the rennet and mix well. Leave
in a cool place to set.

When required, spread over the cream
and sprinkle over the spices and/or the
rose petals.

ELDERFLOWER AND ROSE PETAL SORBET

Elder is a tree of magic and myth, dedicated to the god Thor, sacred to the gypsies, and an emblem of sorrow and death, yet claimed to have great medicinal value. Today, its superstitions and virtues forgotten, the berries are still gathered for rich, dark wine, and the flowers for jams, syllabubs, sorbets, elderflower wine and champagne.

The leaves and petals of the rose was used in medieval kitchens for flavouring junkets, sauces, syllabubs, cakes and salads.

It is a very pretty sweet, and if the glasses are chilled about one hour before serving, a small fresh pink flower placed on top of the sorbet, and a little chilled pink champagne poured over, it is a visual treat as well as a delicious and refreshing sweet.

To serve 6–8

1 litre/2 pints [5 cups] elderflowers, stalks removed and freshly picked
1 litre /2 pints [5 cups] strongly scented rose petals
400 ml/¾ pint [2 cups] cold water
juice and thinly peeled rind [zest] of 2 lemons
2 tbsp triple strength rose water
300 g/10 oz [1¼ cups] caster [superfine] sugar

Put the sugar, water and lemon peel into a saucepan and heat until the sugar has dissolved. Remove from the heat.

Wash the elderflowers and rose petals and put them into the sugar syrup. Allow to infuse for 30 minutes. Strain the syrup through muslin, squeezing all the juice from the flowers and petals.

Discard the flowers and the residue left in the muslin. Add the lemon juice to the syrup, pour in the rose water. Stir to mix, then freeze in a suitable container.

Remove from the freezer about half an hour before serving. By scraping a spoon across the top of the sorbet and not digging into it, a much finer texture is obtained. Decorate with rose petals and elderflowers.

CLEMENTINE CHEESECAKE

'The Cock o' the Green', otherwise known as Alexander M'Kellar, spent his life pretty much on Bruntsfield Links, and was not unfrequently found practising at the 'short holes' by lamp light. His golf-hating wife, annoyed by his all absorbing passion, on one occasion carried his supper and his night-cap to the links. But Mr M'Kellar, blind to satire, observed to his wife that she 'cou'd wait if she likit till the game was dune, but at present he had no time for refreshment'.

Edinburgh Portraits, Kay, from *Sporting Anecdotes*, 'Ellangowan', 1889

Our intrepid golfer may not have been so easily tempted away from his supper, had it included this delicious cheesecake. It is perfect for cricket or golf picnics, or served with tea after a summer's afternoon tennis party.

To serve 6–8

¼ kg/8 oz digestive biscuits [graham
   crackers]
90 g/3 oz caster [superfine] sugar
grated rind [zest] and juice of
   8 clementines or 4 limes
juice of 1 lemon
5 level tsp gelatine [unflavoured gelatin]
   soaked in 4 tbsp water
90 g/3 oz [5 tbsp] unsalted butter
¼ kg/8 oz [1 cup] cottage cheese
125 g/4 oz [½ cup] sour cream or natural
   yoghurt
For decoration
4 clementines, peeled and sliced
100 ml/4 oz [scant ½ cup] whipped cream

Melt the butter in a pan, break up the
digestive biscuits [graham crackers] into
crumbs, then bind the crumbs with the
melted butter. Press the mixture into the
bottom of a loose sided cake tin and allow
to set.

Into a food processor put the cream or
yoghurt, cottage cheese, sugar, rind [zest]
and juice of the clementines, lemon juice,
and blend together until smooth and
thick.

Dissolve the gelatine by standing the
bowl over hot water and heat until all the
gelatine has completely dissolved, pour
into the cheesecake mixture and blend
together.

Pour the mixture into the prepared
cake tin and allow to set. When ready,
remove from the tin and decorate with the
slices of clementine and whipped cream
rosettes.

CRUSHED STRAWBERRY OR
RASPBERRY CREAM

To serve 6

½ kg/1 lb strawberries or raspberries
3 eggs, separated
4 tbsp icing [confectioner's] sugar
90 g/3 oz [scant ½ cup] caster [superfine]
   sugar
4 tbsp any orange flavoured liqueur
¼ litre /10 fl oz whipping cream
2 level tsp gelatine [unflavoured gelatin]

Wash and pick over the fruit, reserving six
berries for decoration. Place the remaining
berries on a dish and sprinkle over the
icing [confectioner's] sugar. Spoon over
the liqueur and leave to stand for 1 hour.
After that time, pureé the fruit in a
blender, then push through a sieve to
remove pips.

Whisk the egg yolks and caster
[superfine] sugar together until very thick.
Gradually, whisk in the fruit puree.

Whip the cream until just holding
shape and fold a quarter of the quantity
into the fruit mixture. Spoon the
remaining cream into a piping bag with a
star nozzle attached and refrigerate.

Dissolve the gelatine by standing the
bowl containing the gelatine in a bowl of
simmering water. When it has completely
dissolved, stir into the fruit mixture.

As the fruit pureé begins to set, whisk
the egg whites until stiff, then fold into the
pureé. Pour the mixture into a glass bowl
or six individual glasses and set in the
refrigerator.

Decorate with the reserved fresh
berries and the cream piped into rosettes
around the edge of the glasses.

SHERRY AND BRANDY SNAP ICE CREAM

Oakley Court was on the Thames, and after a day's racing it was delightful to go on the river and laze about till dinner-time. Trees and bushes over-hung the water providing many shady corners where punts and boats could hide discreetly and sheltered nooks for lovers to sit in peace and seclusion.

Chit-Chat,
Lady Augusta Fane, *c.* 1884

Those were the days when picnics were taken in elegant profusion down on the river. This ice cream would have been ideal. It is also excellent as a dessert for an *al fresco* lunch on the lawn.

To serve 6

½ litre /1 pint [2½ cups] double [heavy] cream
2 sherry glasses good cream sherry
90 g/3 oz [6 tbsp] icing [confectioner's] sugar
¼ kg/8 oz [1 cup] brandy snaps, crushed
125 g/4 oz whipped cream for decoration

Beat the double [heavy] cream gradually adding the sugar and sherry a little at a time. Beat until it just holds its shape in soft peaks. Pour into a loaf tin or individual moulds and freeze overnight.

When required, bring the ice cream from the freezer, turn onto the serving dish and press the crushed brandy snaps all over with a palette knife. Decorate with the whipped cream in rosettes.

If desired, raspberries can accompany this ice cream, or a raspberry sauce.

A VICTORIAN SHERRY AND LEMON SYLLABUB

In Elizabethan times, syllabub was a frothy, milky drink made from milk direct from the cow with cider, wine or ale added. It became a creamy whipped pudding during the eighteenth century.

The juice of fresh fruits may be added either with or without the alcohol.

To serve 6

½ litre /1 pint [2½ cups] double [heavy] cream
125 g/4 oz [1 cup] toasted flaked almonds
3 small wine glasses of sweet or medium sherry
grated rind [zest] and juice of 2 lemons
90 g/3 oz [scant ½ cup] caster [superfine] sugar; this may vary according to the sweetness of the sherry and your guests' palates.

Put the cream into a bowl with the sugar and whisk until it holds its shape. Add the sherry, a glass at a time, beating continuously. Add the rind [zest] and juice of the lemons, fold in two-thirds of the toasted almonds.

Pile the syllabub into a glass bowl or individual glasses. Sprinkle the remaining almonds on top of the bowl or each glass. Stand in a cool place until required.

ATHOLL BROSE (PUDDING)

The word brose is derived from broth, which was made from boiled milk or water and mixed with oatmeal. There are many different versions of this recipe, which can be a drink as well as a rich pudding. There are also many differing stories about how this beverage originated, but one version is that in the fifteenth century, the Earl of Atholl captured the Earl of Ross (who had threatened the Earl of Atholl's daughter) by filling the well at which the Earl of Ross took his water with a mixture of whisky, water and honey. After drinking the Earl of Ross fell into a stupor and was easily captured.

To serve 4

100 ml/4 fl oz [½ cup] whisky
¼ litre /½ pint [1¼ cups] double [heavy] cream
3 tbsp runny heather honey
60 g/2 oz [1 cup] oatmeal, toasted

Whip the double [heavy] cream until it just holds its shape. Stir in the honey and oatmeal, pour in the whisky, mix well, then chill in small stemmed glasses.

When required, remove from the refrigerator and decorate with a twist of lemon and, if available, a small piece of heather.

SCOTS CREAM CROWDIE

In Scotland, crowdie means a home made cheese, similar to cottage cheese though creamier and softer in texture. It was also the name given to the breakfast porridge. Nowadays the name is given to this creamy sweet, which has nothing to do with cheese.

To serve 4–6 depending on size of pots or dishes

½ litre /1 pint [2½ cups] double [heavy] cream
60 g/2 oz [¼ cup] coarse oatmeal
60 g/2 oz [¼ cup] caster [superfine] sugar
1 tbsp rum or whisky
125 g/4 oz fresh raspberries or blackberries

Toss the oatmeal in a thick bottomed saucepan over heat for five minutes. Beat the cream to a thick froth. Stir in the oatmeal, sugar, rum or whisky and the fresh fruit. Serve immediately.

SPICED PEACHES

History reports that King John died of a surfeit of peaches and new cider; we trust this will not be the case here. This recipe is an adaption of an Hannah Glasse receipt of 1747.

To serve 6

100 ml/4 fl oz [½ cup] brandy
6 ripe peaches
1 tsp cinnamon
400 ml/¾ pint [2 cups] water
6 cloves
360 g/12 oz [1½ cups] unrefined granulated sugar (brown)
¼ tsp ground mace

Peel the peaches by putting them into a bowl of boiling water for a few minutes. Drain off the water, and peel: the skin should come away easily. Insert a clove into each peach.

Put the sugar, cinnamon, mace and water into a large pan and bring to the boil, stir well until the sugar has thoroughly dissolved. Drop the peaches into the syrup and gently cook for 20 minutes (this is so the fruit retains its colour in the jar). Check that the peaches are well covered with the syrup.

When ready, remove the peaches and put them into a wide topped jar, a Kilner is ideal. Pour the brandy into the syrup, stir well, and pour into the jar over the peaches. Allow to cool before sealing the jar.

Put into a cool place and leave for at least three to four days before eating.

BILBERRY AND APPLE MERINGUE PIE

Bilberry pie was traditionally made on 12 August to celebrate the start of the grouse-shooting season. This recipe is a variation on the traditional pie with the addition of a meringue topping. Blackberries can be used if bilberries are not available.

To serve 4–6

1 kg/2 lb bilberries, washed
½ kg/1 lb apples, peeled and cored
caster [superfine] sugar to taste
¼ kg/8 oz shortcrust [pie] pastry
4 egg whites
¼ kg/8 oz [1 cup] caster [superfine] sugar

Cook the fruit in about 125 ml/¼ pint [½ cup] of water until soft and fairly thick

Line a pie dish with the rolled out pastry and bake blind in a hot oven until golden brown.

Sweeten the fruit pureé to taste with the sugar and put into the cooked pastry case, spread evenly

Beat the egg whites until very thick, then beat in the caster [superfine] sugar a spoonful at a time until you have a meringue consistency.

Pile the meringue over the fruit and form rough peaks with a fork. Scatter a little extra sugar over the top and put into a moderate oven until the peaks are golden. Serve with thick cream. The cream can be flavoured with a little rum or brandy if desired.

STRAWBERRY AND CREAM
SHORTBREAD

Called in at Hay Castle and went with the four pretty girl archers to shoot and pick up their arrows in the field opposite the castle.

Kilvert's Diaries, 26 June 1872

And then, no doubt, on to tea in the vicarage garden under the shade of an ancient spreading oak tree. Whether for tea in the garden or for a picnic in the country, these strawberry shortbreads are delicious and remind us of those long, warm summer afternoons.

To make 8–10 segments

For the shortbread
130 g/4½ oz [½ cup] caster [superfine] sugar
350 g/12 oz [2 cups] plain [all purpose] flour
225 g/8 oz [1 cup] unsalted butter, room temperature
caster [superfine] sugar for sprinkling
For the strawberry and cream filling
300 ml/½ pint [1¼ cups] whipping cream
250 g/½ lb fresh strawberries, washed and hulled
50–75 g/2–3 oz [approximately ¼ cup] caster [superfine] sugar to sweeten the cream

Pre-heat the oven to 190°C/350°F/Gas Mark 5

To make the shortbread, rub the sugar and butter together, then lightly work in the flour with your finger tips, mixing until the ingredients form a dough. Shape the mixture into a circle about 1.5 cm/½ in. thick, or place inside a flan ring on a greased baking tray. Prick all over using a fork and mark into segments of equal size. You can if desired cut the shortbread into heart shapes; these look very attractive (if cutting the shortbread into shapes, the mixture should be slightly thinner in depth, about a 5 mm/¼ in. or a little less if preferred and baked for only 15 minutes).

Bake in the pre-heated oven for 40 to 45 minutes until a pale golden brown. Allow to cool a little before removing from the baking tray.

Put the shortbread onto a wire rack and sprinkle with the caster [superfine] sugar. Store in an airtight tin until required.

For the filling, whip the cream until it holds its shape, fold in the caster [superfine] sugar to taste.

Slice the strawberries and mix with the cream, reserving a few whole berries for decoration.

Spread the cream and strawberry mixture onto a shortbread segment or heart, put another segment on top. Sprinkle over a little more caster [superfine] sugar, and top with a strawberry, or put one or two whole strawberries around the edge of the shortbread shapes.

TOFFEE MERINGUES

As I approached this spot in the evening about half an hour before sunset, I was surprised to hear the hum of voices, and occasionally a shout of merriment from the meadow beyond the churchyard; which I found, when I reached the stile, to be occasioned by a very animated game of cricket, in which the boys and young men of the place were engaged, while the females and old people were scattered about: some seated on the grass watching the progress of the game, and others sauntering about in groups of two or three, gathering little nosegays of wild roses and hedge flowers.

Cricket on a Sunday from
The Posthumous Papers of the
Pickwick Club
Charles Dickens, 1888

What an idyllic scene Charles Dickens conjures up for our imagination. If we are fortunate enough for this scene to become a reality, what better sweet to take along in the picnic basket than these delicious meringues. They can be put together when required for eating, so they will travel very easily. There are a variety of ways of serving these meringues, crème fraîche can be used instead of thick cream, if a not so rich sweet is desired. The cream can be omitted altogether and just served with the toffee sauce. It is very much a matter of preference.

To make approximately 8 meringues,
depending on spoon size for the
meringues

4 large egg whites
125 g/4 oz [½ cup] caster [superfine] sugar
125 g/4 oz [½ cup] light brown Muscavado sugar
whipped thick cream to sandwich meringues together
silicone bakewell paper [parchment paper] to line the baking tray
For the sauce
90 g/3 oz [6 tbsp] unsalted butter
4 rounded tbsp golden unrefined granulated sugar
6 tbsp golden [corn] syrup
125 ml/¼ pint [½ cup] hot water
juice of ½ lemon
4 tsp cornflour [cornstarch] mixed well with 4 tbsp cold water

Beat the egg whites until very thick. Mix the two sugars together and beat into the egg white mixture 1 tbsp at a time.

Put 2 tsp full of meringue onto the lined baking tray in rows. Make sure the meringue mixture does not touch.

Place in the bottom of the oven at the lowest temperature. They need to 'dry out' rather than cook and should take about 3 hours depending on oven temperature variations. When cooked, allow to cool. They should then come easily away from the paper.

To make the sauce: put the butter, sugar and syrup into a heavy based saucepan. Cook gently until the mixture is a good toffee colour.

Remove from the heat and add the hot water and lemon juice. Add this slowly as the mixture may splash when in contact with the toffee.

Pour in the well-mixed cornflour [cornstarch] and return to the heat. Stir all the time until the mixture thickens.

Remove from the heat and pour into a jug to cool.

When all is ready, sandwich the meringues together with the whipped cream and pour over the toffee sauce. Decorate if desired with a small fresh flower in the centre.

MRS BEETON'S TENNIS CAKE

Long, lazy summer afternoons and tea on the lawn have long been associated with Wimbledon and private tennis parties. The days when the first lady tennis players wore elaborately flounced, ground length dresses, high necks, ornamented sleeves and clinched waists, have long since gone, but tea on the lawns and this cake can still be enjoyed, weather permitting. The recipe comes from the Wimbledon Lawn Tennis Museum.

To serve 6

45 g/1½ oz [¼ cup] candied peel
30 g/1 oz [¼ cup] almonds
180 g/6 oz [¾ cup] butter
180 g/6 oz [¾ cup] granulated sugar
125 g/4 oz [1 cup] raisins
250 g/8 oz [2 cups] plain [all purpose] flour
4 eggs
juice of ½ lemon
grated rind [zest] of 1 lemon
glacé cherries
icing [confectioner's] sugar
angelica

Blanch and chop the almonds (bought chopped almonds can be used). Slice the candied peel thinly and roughly chop the raisins.

Cream the butter and sugar together until pale and fluffy. Lightly whisk the eggs, add half the quantity to the butter and cream mixture and beat well.

Sieve the flour and add to the creamed butter and sugar mixture, fold in the remaining eggs, add the almonds, raisins, peel, lemon rind [zest] and juice. Blend well then put the mixture into a 18 cm/ 7 in. round cake tin, level the top.

Bake in the centre of the oven at 180°C/350°F/Gas Mark 4, for 1–1¼ hours, reduce the temperature to 160°C/325°F/ Gas Mark 3 and cook for a further ½ hour. The cake should be firm to the touch and just beginning to shrink from the sides of the tin.

Allow the cake to cool a little before removing from the tin. When cold, decorate with the icing [confectioner's] sugar sprinkled over the top, cherries and angelica. If preferred, a white icing can be made and spread over the cake.

Tennis Cake.

GOLDEN GINGER CAKE

Table set with linen cloth,
Milk jug filled with creamy froth,
Cucumber sandwiches, bread home
                                        baked,
Sardines and ham, a ginger cake
Good things to eat on a July Sunday.
A July Sunday,
Nikki Rowan-Kedge, 1984

A very light and easy to make cake, ideal
for summer picnics, or tea in the garden.
It can also be decorated to make an
unusually flavoured birthday cake.

To serve 4–6

125 g/4 oz [½ cup] **English butter**
60 g/2 oz [¼ cup] **soft brown sugar**
60 g/2 oz [¼ cup] **demerara sugar**
2 large eggs
3 tbsp golden [corn] syrup
3 tbsp milk
3 tsp ground ginger
90 g/3 oz [scant ½ cup] **chopped walnuts**
150 g/5 oz [1¼ cups] **self raising flour [cake flour plus scant tsp baking powder]**
90 g/3 oz [¾ cup] **wholemeal [whole wheat] flour**
1 tsp baking powder

Beat the butter and two sugars together
until light and creamy. Add the eggs and
syrup and beat well together.

Mix the two flours together with the
baking powder and fold into the butter
and syrup mixture. Add the ginger,
walnuts and milk and mix well using a
metal spoon.

Put the mixture into a loose-sided cake
tin about 15 cm/6 in. round and bake in a
pre-heated oven 160°C/325°F/Gas Mark 3
for 1½ to 1¾ hours.

When ready, allow to cool then spread
over a layer of icing to which has been
added a little ginger syrup. Top with
walnuts.

WHOLEMEAL HONEY HEART BISCUITS [COOKIES]

Philippa made agitated signals to me; I cut
her dead and went to ground in the tea
tent.
Some Experiences of an Irish R.M.,
Somerville and Ross, 1899

Biscuits [cookies] have been around since
Roman times when wheat flour was boiled
to a paste, then left to dry. It was then cut
into pieces, fried and served with honey.
These biscuits are ideal for tea or to put
in one's pocket while out in the sports
field.

To make approximately 24 biscuits, depending on cutter size

150 g/5 oz [10 tbsp] **margarine**
½ kg/1 lb [4 cups] **plain wholemeal [whole wheat] flour**
½ tsp baking powder
60 g/2 oz [¼ cup] **cracked wheat**
1 tsp ground ginger
125 g/4 oz [¼ cup] **thick honey**
150 g/5 oz [scant ½ cup] **golden [corn] syrup**

Sift the flour and baking powder into a
bowl. Mix in the cracked wheat and
ginger.

Put the margarine into a pan, add the

honey and syrup. Heat gently over a low heat until the fat is completely melted, stirring well to combine the ingredients.

Allow to cool, then stir in the flour. Knead the dough well then wrap in cling film [wrap] and leave for 1 hour in the refrigerator. Meanwhile, pre-heat the oven to 180°C/350°F/Gas Mark 4 and grease a baking tray with margarine.

Roll out the dough onto a floured board until about a 5 mm/¼ in. thick. Cut out heart shapes and place on the greased baking tray. Bake in the centre of the oven for roughly 15 minutes or until golden brown.

Remove from the oven and allow to cool on a wire rack.

APRICOT CURD

Last night the rats most provokingly carried off into their hole the contents of two dishes of apricots which had been gathered yesterday for our croquet party today and left on the shelf in the dining room closet.

Kilvert's Diaries, 29 July 1874

We can bless our refrigerators for the fact that this sort of thing doesn't happen too often today. As with all fruit curds, this one will keep for three to four weeks in the refrigerator. It is delicious spread upon home-made bread and is ideal for picnics or for tea after a game of croquet or tennis.

To make about 1 kg/2 lbs

¼ kg/8 oz [1 cup] caster [superfine] sugar
180 g/6 oz [1½ cups] apricots, dried
60 g/2 oz [4 tbsp] butter
2 eggs, beaten
grated rind [zest] and juice of 1 lemon

Cover the apricots with water and soak for 24 hours.

Tip the soaked apricots into a pan and bring to the boil, simmer until tender. This takes about ½ hour. Put the fruit through a coarse sieve or blender.

Put the fruit pulp in a large bowl over boiling water, or in the top of a double saucepan. Add the sugar, grated rind and juice of the lemon and the butter. Cover, and cook over a low heat stirring all the time until the sugar has dissolved.

Remove from the heat and strain the beaten eggs into the apricot pureé.

Return to the heat and cook gently until the curd coats the back of a spoon, stirring from time to time.

Pot in clean jars and seal in the usual way.

AUTUMN

Hungry hunters and shooters, triumphant and bemired from the chase, love to quench their thirst and spoil their dinners under the stuffed heads in the great hall, and golfers and fishermen to magnify their exploits amid the miscellaneous companionship of the hotel lounge. All these confess the hour with grateful pleasure, but the true spiritual home of the tea-pot is surely in a softly-lighted room, between a deep arm chair and a sofa cushioned with Asiatic charm, two cups only, and these of thinnest china, awaiting their fragrant infusion, whilst the clock points nearer to six than five, and a wood fire flickers sympathetically on the hearth.

Tea time from *Kitchen Essays*,
Lady Jekyll, 1921

CHESTNUT AND SMOKED BACON SOUP

Some good advice from Mr Facey Romford: 'Happy are they who go out to please themselves, and not to astonish others.'

Mr Facey Romford's Hounds,
R. S. Surtees, 1865

We should please ourselves very much if we could come home to a hot bowl of this delicious soup. It is easy to make and is transportable in a flask, which would be more than welcome on a cold day out in the country.

To serve 4

1 tin natural chestnut pureé
2 large onions, peeled and finely chopped
1 clove garlic, crushed with a little salt
90 g/3 oz chopped smoked bacon, rind removed
60 g/2 oz [4 tbsp] unsalted butter or 4 tbsp vegetable oil
300 ml/½ pint [scant 1¼ cups] chicken stock
300 ml/½ pint [1¼ cups] single [light] cream
1 tsp chopped parsley
salt and black pepper
fried bread croutons, optional

Melt the oil or butter in a large saucepan, put in the chopped bacon and cook until the fat begins to run, remove the bacon and put to one side.

Put the chopped onion into the saucepan and cook until soft, add the crushed garlic, and cook for a further 3 minutes. Pour in the stock and the chestnut pureé, stir well until free from any lumps. The soup can be put into a food blender at this stage, liquidised, then put back into the saucepan.

Put the chopped bacon back into the pan, season very well, pour in the single [light] cream and simmer gently for a few minutes.

Pour the hot soup into warm soup bowls, sprinkle over chopped parsley and fried bread croutons if used. A swirl of cream can be poured over each soup surface.

MUSHROOM AND GINGER SOUP

This is an ideal soup to take on a picnic or in a thermos for any outdoor pursuit. It is warming and piquant with the addition of ginger, and is very delicious.

To serve 4–6

2 large onions, peeled and chopped
1 clove garlic, crushed with a little salt
3 pieces preserved ginger, chopped
2.5 cm/1 in. piece of root ginger, skin removed, finely grated
¾ litre/1½ pints [3¾ cups] chicken or meat stock
125 g/4 oz [½ cup] unsalted butter
250 g/½ lb mushrooms, washed and sliced
salt and ground black pepper
1 tbsp parsley, chopped for decoration

Melt the butter in a large saucepan, add the onion, garlic and grated root ginger. Cook until the onion becomes golden in colour and is slightly caramelised. Add the mushrooms and the chopped preserved ginger. Stir well, then pour in the stock.

Season well and simmer for about $\frac{3}{4}$ hour.

If a thicker soup consistency is required, a little cornflour [cornstarch] can be used: slacken with four tbsp of water, and then add to the soup, stirring quickly.

Sprinkle over the chopped parsley when ready to serve. Fried bread croutons and a chunk of wholemeal [whole wheat] bread are an excellent accompaniment and make this soup a meal in itself.

If you can, use home-made stock made from lamb, chicken or beef bones boiled. Also use any left over meat juices from the roasting pan.

BROWN WINDSOR SOUP

Of all the items on the menu, soup is that which exacts the most delicate perfection and the strictest attention.

Escoffier (1846–1935)

This soup was reputedly a favourite of Queen Victoria, and frequently topped the bill of fare. It is a delicious soup when properly made, and is not to be confused with the brown tasteless liquid found in some hotels and guest houses.

To serve 6

$\frac{1}{4}$ kg/8 oz shin of beef, diced
1 medium carrot, peeled and chopped
90 g/3 oz [6 tbsp] unsalted butter
1 medium onion, peeled and chopped
1 litre/2 pints [5 cups] beef stock
30 g/1 oz [scant $\frac{1}{4}$ cup] flour
3 tbsp Madeira or medium sherry
1 bouquet garni
salt and black pepper

Melt the butter in a pan and fry the onion and carrot, remove from the pan, put to one side.

Put in the diced beef and brown the meat. Cook until just turning brown, sprinkle in the flour and cook for a further 5 minutes.

Put the carrot and onion back into the pan, pour in the stock and bring to the boil, stirring all the time. Add the bouquet garni, season well and simmer for 2 hours.

Remove the bouquet garni and press the soup through a sieve or liquidise. The soup should be a fairly thick and smooth texture. Re-heat and add the Madeira or sherry.

Check the seasoning and serve with fried bread croutons or hot toast. A swirl of cream on top will add the finishing touch.

HUNTER'S SOUP

The huntsman winds his horn.
The huntsman winds his horn.
And a hunting we will go,
A hunting we will go.

At length his strength to faintness worn,
   Poor Reynard ceases flight;
The hungry, homeward we return,
   To feast away the night.
   Then a drinking we will go,
   A drinking we will go,
   A drinking we will go,
      Coridon's Song and Other Verses,
                   1904

This hearty, stimulating soup can be made from any left over game or scraps of meat. It is ideal for cold days after a day's sport and appetites can match the generosity of the biggest soup bowls. When served with a chunk of wholemeal [whole wheat] bread, it can be a meal in itself.

To serve 4–6

90 g/3 oz [6 tbsp] **unsalted butter or dripping [beef fat]**
125 g/4 oz **streaky bacon, cut into small pieces**
1 litre/2 pint [5 cups] **strong game stock**
250 ml/½ pint [1¼ cups] **good red wine**
1 large **carrot thinly sliced**
4 sticks **celery finely chopped**
1 large **onion peeled and chopped**
180 g/6 oz **game scraps cut into small pieces (previously cooked)**
2 tbsp **plain flour**
salt and pepper

In a large pan, melt the butter or dripping [beef fat], add the vegetables and the pieces of bacon. Cook until golden brown. Add the flour and stir well, taking care not to have the heat too high as it will burn the flour. When the flour is just turning brown, pour in the stock. Stir well and scrape off all the flour from the bottom of the pan so as to incorporate all the flour and flavour. Pour in the wine and season to taste.

   Simmer gently for 3 hours over a low heat. Just before serving, add the pieces of cooked, left over game. Decorate with chopped parsley and fried bread croutons if desired.

TERRINE OF HARE

What a breakfast: pot of hare; ditto of trout, pot of prepared shrimps; dish of plain shrimps; tin of sardines, beautiful beefsteak; eggs, muffins; large loaf, and butter, not forgetting capital tea. There's a breakfast for you.
            Wild Wales,
      George Borrow, 1862

Hares have been eaten in Britain for around five thousand years, but for many, many years were considered an inferior and a poor man's meat. Attitudes changed around the seventeenth century due to various acts of Parliament protecting the hare from extinction and this seems to have given the hare a certain respectability.

   It is now among our cheapest game and is an excellent meat for terrines and patés; it also freezes well. This recipe can be started two days in advance. It can be used as a first course or as the main dish.

Serve with a fresh green salad, redcurrant jelly and wholemeal [whole wheat] bread.

To serve 6

For the terrine
½ kg/1 lb veal, minced
½ kg/1 lb belly of pork [pork sides], minced
meat of 1 hare
350 g/¾ lb streaky bacon, rind removed
1 tsp herbs, i.e., basil, thyme, marjoram, chopped
salt and black pepper
For the marinade
8 juniper berries, crushed
¾ wine glass of brandy
4 bay leaves
1 tsp salt
10 peppercorns

Mix together the marinade ingredients in a large bowl. Cut the meat from the hind legs and the saddle of the hare into thin slices. There should be about ½–¾ kg/1½ lb of meat. Leave the meat to marinade for eight to twelve hours, turning it occasionally.

The following day, mince the veal with the liver and kidneys of the hare, remove any gristle or bones. Remove the rind from the pork and mince.

Line two ½ litre / 1 pint or one 1 litre/2 pint oven-proof dish with the streaky bacon, reserve four slices for the top of the terrine.

Strain the marinade liquid into a bowl, lay half the quantity of veal on the bacon, followed by all the pork. Sprinkle each layer with the herbs and seasonings. Lay the hare meat over the pork, pour the strained marinade liquid over the meat,

top with the remainder of the veal. Season again and sprinkle over the remaining herbs.

Cover the top with the four bacon slices and four to six bay leaves. Cover the terrine with a layer of buttered greaseproof [wax] paper before covering with a lid.

Place the terrine in a roasting dish containing enough boiling water to reach half way up the side of the dish. Cook for 2½ hours, one shelf from the bottom, 190°C/375°F//Gas Mark 5.

A skewer pushed gently into the terrine will tell you if it is ready: the skewer should come away cleanly and the juices run a clear yellow. Twenty minutes before cooking time is completed, remove the lid and greaseproof [wax] paper to allow the top to brown.

Take out of the oven and allow to cool for about 30 minutes, then cover the terrine with clean greaseproof [wax] paper and weight down with a 1 kg/2 lb weight on top of a saucer.

When required, serve with plenty of hot buttered toast.

85

SMOKED HADDOCK AU GRATIN

Splashing along the boggy roads all day
And over brambled hedge and
                              holding clay,
I shall not think of him:
But when the watery fields grow
                        brown and dim,
And hounds have lost their fox, and
                              horses tire,
I know that he'll be with me on the way
Home through the darkness to the
                        evening fire.
Together,
Siegfried Sassoon, 1942

To serve 4–6 as a first course

½ kg/1 lb smoked haddock
1 onion, peeled and chopped
45 g/1½ oz [3 tbsp] unsalted butter
45 g/1½ oz [scant ½ cup] plain [all purpose]
    flour
400 ml/¾ pint [2 cups] milk
1 tbsp chopped parsley
125 ml/¼ pint [½ cup] single [light] cream
125 g/4 oz [scant cup] strong flavoured
    hard cheese, grated
salt and cayenne pepper
3 tsp anchovy essence [extract]

Pour the milk into a pan, add the haddock
and gently poach for 10–12 minutes.
Strain off the milk and reserve for the
sauce. Flake the fish, removing any skin
and bones.

Melt the butter in the pan, add the
onion and cook until soft. Mix in the flour
and stir well, cook for a couple of
minutes. Pour in the milk and beat well
until you have a sauce consistency.
Remove from the heat.

Mix the flaked haddock into the sauce
mixture, add the chopped parsley,
anchovy essence, two-thirds of the cheese,
and the cream. Season well and stir until
all the ingredients are well blended, taking
care not to break up the fish too much.

Put the mixture into your chosen dish,
top with the remaining cheese and put into
a moderate oven 180°C/350°F/Gas Mark
4 for 45 minutes or until golden brown
and bubbling. The cooking time will
depend upon the depth of dish used.

Serve hot from the oven sprinkled with
a little chopped parsley on top.

SAUTÉED GARLIC MUSHROOM CAPS FILLED WITH CHICKEN LIVER PATÉ

'Put off the dinner (wheeze); put off the
dinner (puff),' repeated he, blowing
furiously into his clean shirt-frill, which
stuck up under his nose like a hand-saw;
'put off the dinner (wheeze); put off the
dinner (puff); I wish you wouldn't do such
things without consulting (gasp) me'. . . .
'Well, but, my dear, you know hunters are
always allowed a little law,' observed Mrs
Jog.
Mr Sponge's Sporting Tour,
R. S. Surtees, 1853

I quite agree with Mr Jogglebury Crowdy,
with a first course as delicious and unusual
as this, I too would want to be at it as
soon as possible. Any size mushrooms will
do, but the medium sized ones are
normally sufficient for a first course,
allowing two or three mushrooms per
person. You can of course, if you wish, use
one large horse mushroom.

To serve 4

8 medium or 12 smaller mushrooms
2 small cloves garlic, crushed with a little
    salt
60 g/2 oz [4 tbsp] unsalted butter
500 g/1 lb chicken livers
4 rashers [slices] streaky bacon, chopped
1 clove garlic, crushed with a little salt
1 small onion, peeled and chopped
2 tsp tomato pureé [paste]
2 tsp English mustard
80 ml/3 fl oz [good ¼ cup] vegetable oil
salt and black pepper

Wipe the mushrooms and remove the
stalks. Put the caps into a bowl. Mix the
vegetable oil with the two crushed cloves
of garlic and pour over the mushroom
caps. Season well and allow the garlic oil
to soak into the mushrooms while
preparing the paté.

Melt the butter in the pan and fry the
chopped bacon until the fat begins to run.
Add the chopped onion and crushed
garlic. Chop the mushroom stalks and add
them to the pan. Stir, and cook until the
vegetables are soft, drain and put into a
bowl.

Put the chicken livers into the pan and
sauté briskly until no longer pink. A little
extra butter may be necessary if the pan is
dry. Add the tomato pureé [paste] and
mustard, season and mix well together.
Remove from the pan and put with the
previously cooked vegetables.

Put the liver and vegetable mixture
into a food processor and blend until
smooth and creamy.

Put the oil soaked mushroom caps
onto a baking tray or into a grill [broiler]
pan, spoon the blended paté onto each

mushroom. Mill a little black pepper over
each cap and grill [broil] or bake in a
moderate oven for 20 minutes. The time
will vary according to size of mushroom
cap, so a constant check will be necessary
to prevent over-cooking and burning.

If desired and you have the time, half
a slice of fried bread, cut into a round or
heart shape, can be put under each
mushroom.

Decorate with sprigs of fresh parsley.

BEEF-STEAK AND KIDNEY PIE

In medieval times, a 'coffin' of pastry (so called because its shape resembled the macabre box) was made from flour, broth, butter and eggs. They were filled with a mixture of meat and spices and were made on a vast scale to feed large households.

This old English pie is a great favourite of the well-known showjumper Paddy McMahon, but it must have lashings of good gravy.

In this recipe we have used rump steak as it gives a good flavour but you can of course use chuck steak. Also to enhance the flavour, when buying the mushrooms, if possible, buy the black gilled ones, as they make the nicest gravy, dark and rich.

To serve 4

½ kg/1 lb rump or chuck [porterhouse] steak, cut into cubes
60 g/2 oz [4 tbsp] unsalted butter
¼ kg/8 oz black gilled mushrooms
1 large onion, peeled and sliced
2 tbsp seasoned flour
¼ litre /½ pint [1¼ cups] beef stock
salt and black pepper
360 g/12 oz kidney: ox, pig or lamb
1 egg, beaten
360 g/12 oz puff pastry
1 tbsp plain flour

Melt the butter in a pan and cook the onion until soft. Transfer the onion to a dish.

Trim any fat from the diced steak and dip the pieces into the seasoned flour. Put the steak cubes into the pan and lightly brown, adding a little more butter if required. Remove from the pan and put with the onion.

Slice the kidney quite thinly, remove any skin or fat and dip the kidney slices into the seasoned flour. Sauté lightly in the pan with the butter. Remove from the pan and put with the steak and onion. Slice the mushrooms and mix with the steak and kidney. Put the meat and mushrooms into a pie dish.

In the frying pan, put the plain flour and the stock and stir well with a wooden spoon. Cook for a few minutes stirring all the time until the sauce has thickened slightly. Pour into the steak and kidney, just enough to cover.

With kitchen foil, tightly cover the dish and cook in a pre-heated oven for 2½ hours, at 150°C/300°F/Gas Mark 2. During cooking time, check to see if a little more stock is required to top up the dish.

When cooked, remove from the oven and allow to cool. This stage can be prepared well in advance, then only the pastry needs to be added when required.

Pre-heat the oven to 230°C/450°F/Gas Mark 8.

Roll out the pastry and lay it over the steak and kidney. If desired decorate with pastry leaves or strips of pastry. Glaze with the beaten egg.

Bake in the oven for 10 minutes, then reduce the heat to 180°C/350°F/Gas Mark 4, and cook for a further 25 minutes until the pastry is golden brown.

Serve with a pureé of potato and celeriac [celery root] creamed together with butter, cream, salt and white pepper, Brussels sprouts and carrots.

STEAK AND KIDNEY PUDDING

After such a day, the huntsman returns home, feeds his hounds, then has a cup of tea. Returning to the kennel, he sees to any hounds which are lame after the day's work, then returns to his house for dinner. As soon as he tastes his first forkful of steak and kidney pudding, the telephone rings and keeps ringing for most of the evening.

The Huntsman's Day – by an Old Pro
from *The Second Field Bedside Book*, 1969

To serve 6 good appetites

¼ kg/8 oz kidney, cored and skinned
¾ kg/1½ lb stewing or rump steak
¾ kg/1½ lb suet crust pastry (see p. 94)
¼ kg/8 oz mushrooms, wiped and trimmed
400 ml/¾ pint [2 cups] strong stock
45 g/1½ oz [scant ½ cup] seasoned flour
salt and black pepper
a little oil for frying the steak and kidney

Trim the steak of any fat or skin, and cut into slices. Flatten each slice by beating it with a rolling pin. Dice the prepared kidney. Line a well greased pudding basin with the suet crust pastry, allowing enough for a circle to form the lid.

Shake the pieces of steak in the seasoned flour. Heat the oil in a frying pan and fry the pieces of meat until just turning brown, to seal in the meat juices. Remove from the pan and add the kidney, fry quickly for a couple of minutes, remove from the pan.

Quickly fry the prepared mushrooms for about one minute, then remove and put with the steak and kidney into the suet lined basin.

Add the juices from the frying pan to the stock and pour in sufficient stock to cover the meat and mushrooms. Any remaining stock should be reserved for topping later and for serving with the pudding.

Place the suet crust lid firmly on top of the pudding, sealing with a little cold water to ensure a secure edge. Cover the basin tightly with greaseproof [wax] paper or buttered foil. Place a small plate or a saucer over the top.

Stand the basin in a large saucepan with sufficient water to come halfway up the side of the basin. Bring the water to the boil and steam the pudding for 3 hours. Top up with more boiling water from time to time. Do not let the water go off the boil during cooking time.

When cooked, bring the remaining stock to the boil. Remove the pudding from the pan, make a small hole in the pudding top and pour in a little of the boiling stock. Wrap the basin in a white napkin or clean linen tea towel and serve with the remaining stock (if any left), creamed, peppered potatoes, buttered carrots or swedes.

POTTED BEEF

At the summit of the Pike there was not
a breath of air to stir even the papers
which we spread out containing our food.
There we ate our dinner in summer
warmth; and the stillness seemed to be not
of this world.

An Excursion up Scawfell Pike,
Dorothy Wordsworth, 1818

In Scotland, this dish is known as 'Potted
Hough', and was very popular in the
eighteenth and nineteenth centuries.
Potting is one of the oldest methods of
preserving foods of many kinds, and is a
very convenient and easy way of
transporting food for a picnic, for lunch
on a grouse shoot on the moors or for a
fishing expedition. It can also be carried
efficiently by post.

To serve 4

½ kg/1 lb shin of beef
a large beef shin bone, about 1 kg/2 lb
6 black peppercorns
8 allspice berries
1 small bay leaf
3 tbsp salt
1 tsp white pepper

Put the shin bone and meat into a pan,
cover with cold water (approximately 1½
litre/3 pints). Bring to the boil then reduce
the heat and simmer for 3 hours or until
the meat is really tender.

Remove the meat and shin bone from
the liquid and cut off the meat, if any,
from the bone. Cut the beef into pieces, or
if a smoother texture is required, put
through a mincer.

Put the bone back into the pan, add
the salt, bay leaf, peppercorns and
allspice, boil rapidly until the liquid is
reduced by half.

Put the meat into a large bowl or two
smaller bowls and pour in the stock.
Allow to set, then turn out onto your
serving dish or dishes.

HUNTING BEEF

During the Victorian era an enormous
round of beef would decorate the hunt
breakfast sideboard. After eating their fill,
the huntsman would take a large piece of
beef and put it between chunks of bread
to be tucked into a pocket for later in the
day. We hope the Reverend William
Pochin followed this practice on the day
that he became unseated when following
the Cottesmore; he was 'left where he fell'
because he wouldn't be wanted till
Sunday.

To make 15–20 servings

3 kg/6 lb brisket or silverside of beef
30 g/1 oz [scant ¼ cup] soft brown sugar
2 bay leaves, crumbled
360 g/12 oz [2 cups] sea salt
2 cloves
¼ tsp ground mace
7½ g/¼ oz saltpetre
300 ml/½ pint [1¼ cups] dark ale,
    Wadsworth's, Old Peculiar or Guinness

Put the beef joint into a large bowl. Mix
all the dry ingredients together and rub
into the beef. Leave for 2 days in a cool
place, rubbing the meat every day with
this salt mixture. Leave for a further week

to ten days, turning the meat every day. After this time, rinse the beef under cold water and then place it in a saucepan with the beer, add just enough water to cover, bring to the boil and simmer for 5 hours, until the meat is really tender. The beef can be served hot with fresh vegetables or allowed to cool for sandwiches or salads.

MELTON MOWBRAY PORK PIES

Harriette Wilson records that in Leicestershire she was invited to dine every day at the Old Club, originally Lord Forester's house. 'The house was very comfortable and their dinners most excellent. . . . The members led what I considered a very stupid sort of life. They were off at six in the morning . . . and came back to dinner at six. . . . The evening hunt dress is red, lined with white, and the buttons and whole style of it are very becoming. I could not help remarking that the gentlemen never looked half so handsome anywhere in the world as when, glowing with health, they took their seats at dinner, in the dress and costume of the Melton Hunt.'

Memoirs of Harriette Wilson, 1825

The best known Leicestershire pies come from Melton Mowbray, and were traditionally hand shaped in a 'coffer' or 'coffyn'. It was customary to serve these pies for Sunday breakfast, and in some places this custom is still kept up.

To make 4 pies

Hot water crust pastry
125 g/4 oz [½ cup] lard

½ kg/1 lb [4 cups] plain [all purpose] flour
¼ litre /½ pint [1¼ cups] hot water
pinch of salt
1 egg, beaten, to brush over the pastry
For the filling
1 kg/2 lb shoulder of pork. Keep bones and trimmings for stock
¼ tsp ground black pepper
1 tsp salt
¼ tsp ground allspice
3 tsp gelatine [unflavoured gelatin] dissolved in 3 tbsp hot water
½ tsp cayenne pepper
1 tsp anchovy essence [extract]
For the stock
1 stick celery
1 chopped onion
1 bay leaf
1 sage leaf
bones and pork trimmings
water to cover

To make the pastry cases, sift the flour and salt into a warmed mixing bowl, make a well in the centre.

Put the lard into a saucepan with the ¼ litre/½ pint [1¼ cups] hot water and bring to the boil. When the fat has melted, pour into the flour and salt. Mix well together with your hands until smooth and without cracks. Take care not to over handle or the pastry will become greasy as the fat melts from the heat of your hands.

Divide the pastry into four, shape three-quarters of each piece around four floured ½ kg/1 lb jam jars. Do this while the pastry is still fairly warm and pliable. Keep the remaining pastry in a polythene [polyethelene] bag and reserve for the pie lids.

Allow the pastry coffyns to set in a refrigerator until firm, then gently ease them away from the jam jars and place the cases onto a baking tray. Take the remaining pastry, and shape four lids.

To make the pie filling, bone and dice the pork. Put the bones and meat trimmings into a saucepan of water along with the chopped celery, chopped onion, bay and sage leaf and simmer for a good 2 hours to make a good flavoured strong stock.

Toss the diced meat into the spice and mixed seasonings, mix well and pack the mixture into the pie cases. Cover with the pastry lids and dampen the edges, pinch together firmly to make a standing edge, or cut into a turret shape. Brush the tops with the beaten egg, and make a small hole for a steam vent.

Bake in a hot oven 425°F/220°C/Gas Mark 7 for 30 minutes, then reduce the temperature to 350°F/180°C/Gas Mark 4, and cook for a further $1\frac{1}{2}$ hours.

Take 6 tablespoons of the stock (if it has jellied, warm a little so it is easier to pour), add the dissolved gelatine, mix well then pour the stock into the cold pies when ready. Fill the pies as much as they will hold and leave to set.

Serve with hot, buttered toast and home-made chutney.

HAM IN MUSTARD SAUCE

'Won't you take a little refreshment?' asked Mr Springwheat, in the hearty way these hospitable fellows welcome everybody. 'Yes I will,' replied Sponge, turning to the sideboard as though it were an inn. 'That's a monstrous fine ham,' observed he; 'why doesn't somebody cut it?'

'Let me help you to some, sir,' replied Mr Springwheat, seizing the buck-handled knife and fork, and diving deep into the rich red meat with the knife.

Mr Sponge's Sporting Tour,
R. S. Surtees, 1853

To serve 8

16 slices thinly cut ham
$\frac{1}{2}$ litre /1 pint [$2\frac{1}{2}$ cups] béchamel sauce
2 heaped tbsp made mustard (English)
1 heaped tbsp grated Cheddar cheese
3 tbsp double [heavy] cream

Make a paste from the grated cheese, mustard and cream, add it to the béchamel sauce, mix well.

Arrange the slices of ham in an ovenproof dish and pour over the sauce. Top with a little more grated cheese and brown under the grill or in a hot oven.

VEAL AND HAM PIE

An irritable looking man in a tweed suit and leggings went into the village poultry store and asked for a brace of pheasants. 'Sorry, sir,' said the shop-keeper, 'completely sold out of pheasants. I could let you have a nice veal and ham pie though.' 'That's no good,' snapped the customer angrily, 'how could I go home and say I'd shot a veal and ham pie?'

Sporting and Dramatic Yarns,
R. J. B. Sellar, 1925

What can one say? Let us just enjoy this pie which should console any unlucky shooter.

To serve 4

125 g/4 oz lean ham cut into strips
1 large onion, peeled and quartered
4 cloves
1 tsp fresh herbs, e.g., lemon thyme,
    tarragon, parsley etc.
2 hard boiled eggs (optional)
$\frac{1}{2}$ kg/1 lb pie veal cut into cubes
$\frac{1}{2}$ kg/1 lb shortcrust [pie] pastry
salt and white pepper

Pre-heat the oven to 200°C/400°F/Gas
    Mark 6

Trim the veal and remove any skin and
fat, put into a saucepan with the onion
and cloves. Pour over just sufficient water
to cover the meat. Cook gently for 1$\frac{1}{2}$
hours until the veal is tender.

Drain off the liquid into a bowl and
reserve, discard the cloves and put the veal
into another bowl. Add the strips of ham
to the veal along with the herbs and
seasonings. If you are using the hard
boiled eggs, chop them roughly and add to
the meat and herbs. Mix well together
then put into a deep pie dish.

Boil the veal and onion liquid until
reduced by half, pour over the meat.
Allow to cool before covering with pastry

Roll out the pastry and cut a thin strip
to lay around the edge of the pie dish. Lay
the remaining pastry over the pie to form
a lid. Brush all over with beaten egg,
especially around the edges, press the edge
of the pastry firmly to seal.

Decorate if desired with pastry leaves
and bake in the pre-heated oven at the top
for 25 minutes until the pastry is crisp and
cooked, then cover the pie with foil and
move to a lower shelf and cook for a
further 15 minutes.

PLOUGH PUDDING (SAVOURY)

Dorothy Hartley writes in her book *Food
in England* that this savoury roly-poly
used to be made for stable lads' suppers.
It is very delicious and warming,
especially with the addition of the honey
or syrup which makes for a delicious
gravy broth that drips out when cutting
the roll.

'Take a lightly made suet-crust, and roll
out to three-quarters of an inch thick –
cover closely with strips of bacon (cut
across the rasher), try to arrange lean and
fat strips alternately, cover these with
finely chopped onion, a fine sprinkling of
sage, "and pretty well" of white pepper
and a single trail of honey or syrup (a
great improvement to the gravy broth that
should drip out when cutting the roll).'

For a faster cooking time, the onion
and bacon can be fried beforehand and
allowed to cool before putting onto the
suet crust pastry. Roll up, with the join
underneath and cook as for jam roly-poly
(see p. 146), 40 minutes in a pre-heated
oven, 425°F/220°C/Gas Mark 7. If the suet
crust browns too quickly, lower the heat
to 400°F/200°C/Gas Mark 6.

Serve with mushrooms in a mustard
cream sauce.

Raised Pie.

SUET CRUST PASTRY

Suet crust is a very old traditional English pastry, used for savoury and sweet puddings, steamed or boiled. Shredded suet is available from all good supermarkets and grocery stores. Best results though are obtained by using, if possible, fresh beef suet.

Sufficient for a 1.25 litre/2 pint pudding

125 g/4 oz [$\frac{1}{2}$ cup] shredded suet
125 ml/$\frac{1}{4}$ pint [$\frac{1}{2}$ cup] water (approx)
$\frac{1}{2}$ level tsp salt
$\frac{1}{4}$ kg/8 oz [2 cups] self-raising flour or
$\frac{1}{4}$ kg/8 oz [2 cups] plain [all purpose] flour
    with 3 level tsp baking powder

Sift the flour and salt into a bowl, along with the baking powder if used.

If using fresh suet, remove any skin if the butcher has not already done so, chop finely and add to the flour. Ready shredded suet should be just added to the flour straight from the packet. Mix together the suet and the flour thoroughly.

Stir in sufficient water to form a light elastic dough. When the right consistency has been achieved, turn the dough out onto a floured board and knead with the finger tips.

Shape the dough into a ball, put onto a plate, cover, and allow to rest for at least 10–15 minutes. The ingredients for the filling can be prepared during this time.

A ROMANCE OF DUCK WITH APPLES AND ALMONDS

To serve 2

1 duckling, plucked and drawn
125 ml/$\frac{1}{4}$ pint [$\frac{1}{2}$ cup] double [heavy] or
    sour cream
2 tsp crab apple jelly or redcurrant jelly
juice of 1 lemon
small bottle of still apple juice
For the stuffing
90 g/3 oz [6 tbsp] unsalted butter
125 g/4 oz [good cup] wholemeal [whole
    wheat] breadcrumbs
$\frac{1}{4}$ kg/$\frac{1}{2}$ lb good flavoured apples, peeled
    and cored
2 tsp soft brown sugar
grated rind [zest] of 1 lemon
1 small onion, peeled and chopped
90 g/3 oz [$\frac{3}{4}$ cup] lightly toasted slivered
    almonds
1 egg beaten
salt and freshly milled black pepper
2 tsp chopped fresh parsley and thyme

Pre-heat the oven to 180°C/350°F/Gas
    Mark 4

Rub the duck all over with salt and put into a roasting dish, put to one side while you make the stuffing.

Melt the butter in a large pan, then add the chopped onion and apple, sauté until just turning brown. When ready, put this into a mixing bowl. Add the breadcrumbs, half the amount of slivered almonds, sugar, lemon rind [zest], herbs, salt and pepper and the beaten egg. Bind well together. When well mixed, fill the duck with the stuffing and roast, 20 minutes to the $\frac{1}{2}$ kg/1lb.

Half an hour before the completed cooking time, remove the duck from the oven and pour over the apple juice.

When cooked, remove once more from the oven and spoon away any fat from the meat juices. Pour these duck juices into a saucepan or remove the duck from the roasting pan, and cook the juices in the roasting dish over a gentle heat. Add the jelly and lemon juice to the duck juices and stir well, getting all the residue from the bottom of the pan.

Carve the duck into four joints and arrange the stuffing in the centre. Add the cream to the sauce, stir gently and put into a sauce-boat.

Sprinkle the remaining slivered almonds over the duck, decorate with a few sprigs of fresh parsley and serve.

An apple and walnut salad would go well with this dish, and new potatoes.

SMOKED CHICKEN AND ALMOND SALAD WITH A HONEY AND WALNUT VINAIGRETTE DRESSING

The morning after his arrival he announced that he was leaving that day, and on being asked the reason Mr Hibbert replied: 'I am leaving because the "side dishes" [entrees] were so cold at supper they made my teeth ache all night.'

Chit-Chat,
Lady August Fane, *c.* 1884

Shooting parties are very serious affairs, and have to be arranged months beforehand; if a guest fails at the last moment, the excuse has to be a very good one indeed. Maybe if Mr Washington Hibbert had had this salad, there might not have been any complaints. It is a very different and unusual salad, refreshing and piquant with its honey vinaigrette dressing – easy to prepare, too.

To serve 6

1 smoked chicken, approximately 1¼ kg/ 2½ lbs, skinned, boned and thinly sliced
90 g/3 oz [½ cup] flaked almonds, lightly toasted
any fresh mixed salad: endive, raddicio, lambs' lettuce, watercress
For the dressing
1 clove garlic, crushed with a little salt
2 tbsp liquid honey
5 tbsp tarragon vinegar
8 tbsp walnut oil
4 tbsp vegetable oil
juice of ½ lemon
salt and black pepper

Put all the dressing ingredients into a large screw-topped jar and shake until well-blended and creamy to look at.

Toss the chicken slices with the cleaned and prepared salad leaves. Sprinkle over the almonds and pour over the dressing. Toss again and serve with crusty home-made bread.

VENISON AND BEEF CARBONADE

Ashen green the deer-park stretches
                              up to where
Shaven lawns are thronged and
                              gaily bright;
Scarlet-coated horsemen hail another
                              year,
Grouped around the pack of
                  dappled white.

January Day
from *Hunter's Morn*,
Edric G. Roberts

The season for venison is variable
according to place and the type of deer.
The best way to cook venison, unless it is
really young, is to marinade it for several
hours or overnight in red wine, a little
olive oil, a few crushed peppercorns, two
tablespoon's wine vinegar, orange peel
and a little salt. A bouquet garni can be
added if desired.

The secret of this carbonade is to use
a really rich dark beer, such as
Theakston's 'Old Peculiar', Wadworth's
'Old Timer' or Guinness.

To serve 6–8

½ kg/1 lb stewing beef
½ kg/1 lb stewing venison
125 g/4 oz streaky bacon, cut into pieces
2 onions, peeled and chopped
1 large clove garlic, crushed with a little
    salt
2 tsp tomato pureé [paste]
½ litre/1 pint good dark beer; red wine can
    be used if preferred
1 tin consommé
2 tbsp redcurrant jelly
2 heaped tbsp plain flour
beef dripping or vegetable oil for
    browning the meat
salt and ground black pepper

Cut the meat into small squares, heat the
fat in a large pan and brown the meat in
the fat a little at a time until it is evenly
browned. Put the browned meat into a
large casserole dish.

Fry the pieces of bacon in the fat and
cook until the bacon fat begins to run,
then add to the meat. Put the onion and
crushed garlic into the frying pan and
cook until the onion is just turning brown.
Add to the casserole.

Put the flour into the frying pan and
cook, stirring all the time for about 2 to
3 minutes. Pour in the beer or wine and
stir well together. Add the consommé and
bring the whole to the boil. Add the
tomato pureé [paste], redcurrant jelly and
the seasonings.

Mix the ingredients together well then
pour the sauce over the meat in the
casserole, cover and cook in a moderate
oven for 2½ to 3 hours.

This casserole improves by keeping for
a day and re-heating when required. Serve
with creamed, peppered potatoes and any
fresh green vegetable and carrots.

VENISON AND KIDNEY
SUET PUDDING

... coming to a part of the forest that ran
into rocks and sandy heathery hills, he
[Mr Jorrocks] threw himself upon his
back on a large flat stone, and, kicking up
first one leg and then the other, to let the
bog water out of his boots, moaned and
groaned audibly. Beginning at a guinea, he

96

bid up to a hundred and twenty to be back at Handley Cross. . . .

Handley Cross,
R. S. Surtees, 1843

And would have bid a lot more no doubt for a suet pudding filled with venison and kidney, washed down with a pint of porter or a bumper or two of claret.

This savoury pudding is marvellous for those chill, cold days. It also looks wonderful when wrapped round with a white napkin for guests to help themselves. Serve with peppered, creamed potatoes, Brussels sprouts and buttered parsnips.

To serve 4

$\frac{1}{4}$ kg/8 oz suet crust pastry
350 g/$\frac{3}{4}$ lb venison cut into small cubes
125 g/$\frac{1}{4}$ lb kidney
2 level tbsp seasoned flour

1 large onion, finely chopped
3 tbsp gravy or stock
ground black pepper

Grease a $\frac{3}{4}$ litre/$1\frac{1}{2}$ pint pudding basin. Cut off a quarter of the pastry for a lid and roll the remaining pastry and line the basin.

Toss the venison cubes in the seasoned flour, sprinkle liberally with ground black pepper. Remove any cores from the kidney, cut into small pieces and add them to the venison. Add the chopped onion and mix well together.

Pack the meat and onion into the lined basin and pour in the gravy or stock. Roll the remaining pastry and form a lid. Dampen the edges with water and press firmly to seal in the meat.

Cover with greaseproof [wax] paper with a fold in the centre to allow for rising. Repeat with a piece of kitchen foil. Tie firmly with string and steam for at least four hours.

VENISON SAUSAGES WITH CUMBERLAND SAUCE

There was a door into an old chapel;
which had been long disused for devotion;
but in the pulpit, as the safest place, was
always to be found a cold chine of beef,
a venison-pasty, a gammon of bacon, or a
great apple-pye, with thick crust, well
baked. He lived to be a hundred; never
lost his eye-sight, nor used spectacles. He
got on horse-back without help; and rode
to the death of a stag, till he was past
fourscore.

Mr Hastings,
William Gilpin (1724—1804)

I wonder if our vicar would appreciate his
pulpit festooned with venison sausages,
perhaps not; these sausages are delicious
and can be bought from good game
dealers or butcher's shops. They are not
too difficult to make if you have the time
and are well worth the effort. The skin for
making sausages may not be too easy to
find, though some butchers may order it
for you. If skins are not available or
required, this mixture can be made into
shapes without skin. They will not hold
their shape as well, but this will not
detract visually or from their flavour.

During Queen Victoria's reign,
Cumberland sauce was almost always
served with game and meat dishes. It was
specially favoured at hunt breakfasts in
Leicestershire, accompanying pheasant or
partridge. With its unique piquant flavour
this sauce is a good companion to venison,
either with the sausages as given above, or
with roast venison in the place of the usual
redcurrant jelly.

To make 20–24 sausages

1 kg/2 lb uncooked venison, finely minced
350 g/12 oz [1½ cups] shredded suet
¼ kg/8 oz [3 cups] fresh wholemeal [whole
    wheat] breadcrumbs
½ tsp grated nutmeg
½ tsp powdered thyme
½ tsp powdered marjoram
2 level tsp salt
1 tsp white pepper
sausage skin if required
For the sauce, to serve between 8–10
½ bottle good port
½ kg/1 lb redcurrant jelly
½ tsp cayenne pepper
grated rind [zest] and juice of 2 oranges
    and 2 lemons
2 tbsp Worcestershire sauce
a pinch of salt

To make the sausages, put all the
ingredients into a large bowl and mix
thoroughly, making sure that all the herbs
and seasonings are well blended.

Form the mixture into sausage or patty
shapes. To put the mixture into skins, take
a forcing bag with a long, wide, nozzle.
Knot one end of a length of sausage skin
(the skin would probably be around
90 cm/3 ft long). Place the other end of the
skin over the nozzle and push the nozzle
in until the nozzle is as close to the knot
as possible. Force the mixture into the
skin, carefully drawing the filled skin
away from the nozzle. Do not overfill or
the sausages will burst. Knot the open end
of the skin and twist the filled skin to form
sausages, at about 8 cm/3 in intervals. Fry
or grill [broil] in the usual way.

For the sauce, put the redcurrant jelly and port into a saucepan, cook until reduced by about one-third. Add all the other ingredients to the pan, remove from the heat and allow to cool.

Put into a clean screw-top jar. The sauce should keep for around two months under refrigeration.

ROAST PHEASANT

Pheasant poaching was fairly common in England, esecially in the summer when the cock bird invades the cottage gardens to sneak the peas. He could be caught quietly with a paper bag and raisins – 'Smear the paper cone inside with treacle of gum, put a few raisins at the bottom, and prop the bag up amongst the peas. When he sticks his head in he cannot see where to go, so he stands still till you fetch him.'

Food in England,
Dorothy Hartley, 1954

Fortunately today we do not need to poach our pheasants as they are available in most supermarkets, butchers' and game dealers' shops. If we are very lucky, there may be an estate nearby whereby we can obtain our game birds easily.

The pheasant should be well hung, anything from three to ten days depending on age of bird, weather and temperature. Most good game dealers and butchers will pluck and dress the pheasant for a modest fee.

To serve 2

1 **pheasant, well hung, plucked and**
   dressed ready for the oven
4 **slices smoky bacon**
3 **tbsp unsalted butter**
To serve with the pheasant:
redcurrant jelly
fried brown breadcrumbs
bread sauce
game chips (potato crisps [chips] heated in
   the oven for emergencies)

Pre-heat the oven 190°C/375°F/Gas
   Mark 5

Spread half the quantity of butter inside the pheasant and the remaining half all over the outside of the bird. Place the bacon slices across the breast. Rub salt and black pepper over the bacon and pheasant.

Roast in the oven, allowing 20 minutes to the pound, hence, a 1½ kg/3 lb bird will take 1 hour. The last 10 minutes of roasting, remove the bacon slices to allow the breast to brown.

The bacon slices can be grilled [broiled] until crisp and then crumbled over the cooked pheasant as a garnish. Serve with the fried breadcrumbs, redcurrant jelly, bread sauce and game chips.

POACHER'S SUET PUDDING

Success to every gentleman that lives in
                Lincolnshire,
Success to every poacher that wants
                to sell a hare,
Bad luck to every game-keeper that
                will not sell his deer,
O 'tis my delight on a shining night,
                in the season of the year.
       The Lincolnshire Poacher, old song

To serve 4–6

180 g/6 oz [$\frac{3}{4}$ cup] **shredded suet**
350 g/12 oz [3 cups] **self-raising flour [cake
    flour plus 2$\frac{1}{4}$ tsp baking powder],
    mixed with a pinch of salt**
$\frac{1}{2}$ kg/1 lb **game meat of your choice, cut
    into small pieces**
$\frac{1}{4}$ kg/8 oz **bacon joint, collar [smoked
    shoulder roll], soaked overnight in
    cold water**
2 **onions, peeled and chopped**
2 **small cooking apples, peeled, cored and
    chopped**
1 **carrot, peeled and chopped**
1 **small bottle cider**
salt and black pepper

Sift the flour and salt into a large bowl and
mix in the suet. Pour in sufficient water to
make a dough. Knead gently on a floured
board. Roll out two-thirds of the dough
and line a greased 1 litre/2 pint pudding
basin. Reserve the remainder for the
cover.

    Into a large bowl put the pieces of
game meat. Chop up the soaked bacon
and add to the game meat, mix together.
Into the lined basin, put layers of the
meat, apple, carrot and onion. Season
each layer well. Pour in the cider,
sufficient to cover the filling.

    Roll out the remaining dough and
form a cover. Dampen the edges and lay
on top of the pudding. Seal well.

    Cover with foil or greaseproof [wax]
paper, putting a pleat in the centre, tie
firmly with string. Put the basin into a pan
with enough water to come half way up
the sides of the basin. Keep the water
boiling, and add more if necessary. Boil
for 4 hours (if the game meat is from an
old bird, rabbit or deer, the cooking time
may be extended; alternatively, the meat
can be cooked before putting into the
basin).

    When ready, serve hot, with a white
napkin wrapped around the basin.

SCALLOPS IN WHITE WINE

A delicious fish course, kindly given by Captain Wallace, who is just as good a gourmet as he is a sportsman. The season for fresh scallops begins in Britain in October, so this is an excellent dish for the start of the hunting season.

To serve 4

4 large scallops (1 per person)
150 ml/¼ pint [½ cup] dry white wine
125 g/4 oz button mushrooms
1 bay leaf
1 slice lemon
30 g/1 oz [2 tbsp] unsalted butter
500 g/1 lb potatoes, peeled and sliced
For the sauce
30 g/1 oz [¼ cup] plain flour
30 g/1 oz [2 tbsp] unsalted butter
2 egg yolks
2 tbsp double [heavy] cream
salt and black pepper
sprig of parsley, chopped for garnishing

Slide the scallops from the shells, wash well under running water. Remove the black beard and intestines. Cut each scallop into 4–6 pieces.

Wipe and thinly slice the mushrooms, put them, with the scallops into a pan with 300 ml/½ pint [1¼ cups] of water; add the wine, lemon slice and bay leaf, cover and simmer for 20 minutes.

Strain, and set aside half of the fish liquid for the sauce. Remove the bay leaf and lemon slice, keep the scallops and mushrooms hot.

Put the potatoes on to boil, while making the sauce.

Melt the butter in a saucepan over a low heat, stir in the flour and cook for a few minutes. Gradually add in the fish liquid, stirring all the time until the mixture is smooth. Bring to the boil, then simmer for 3 minutes. Add the mushrooms and scallops, season to taste. Reheat gently.

Lightly mix the egg yolks and cream together, remove the fish from the heat and stir in the eggs and cream. Put to one side.

When the potatoes are cooked, cream and season. Take a large piping bag and a rosette nozzle, put into it some creamed potato and pipe a border around the edge of the scallop shells. Brush with melted butter and put the shells under the grill [broiler] to brown the potato.

Spoon the scallop and mushroom mixture into the centre of each shell and sprinkle over the chopped parsley.

If desired, the dish can be served as a main course, allowing 3–4 scallops per person, and using plates instead of shells. Either fresh vegetables or boiled rice would be a good accompaniment to this dish.

IRISH WHISKEY FLAMED HERRINGS

The term 'red herring' as a means of diversion dates from the seventeenth century, when the strong-smelling herring was used to lay a false trail to take hounds off a scent.

The fish does need to be soaked really well, for at least thirty minutes before cooking to get rid of the briny taste from the cure. Leave them to soak in boiling water for the time mentioned should be long enough, but you can check by breaking off a piece of fish to taste.

To serve 4

3 tbsp Irish whiskey
4 smoked red herrings
125 g/4 oz [½ cup] unsalted butter

Put the herrings into a saucepan, cover with boiling water and simmer for 3 to 5 minutes. Remove from the water, split the fish lengthways and remove the heads, skin and bones.

Melt the butter in a frying pan and fry the herring fillets for a few minutes, turning once.

Arrange the fillets on a shallow flame-proof dish.

Put the whiskey into a small saucepan and heat gently.

At the table, pour the whiskey over the fish and with a match, ignite. Serve with hot, buttered toast or with well seasoned creamed potatoes. A little cayenne pepper can be sprinkled over the herrings, toast or potatoes.

STILTON TARTLET

For eight years, James Teacher tried to control the hard-riding Quorn field; to revive those memories, he thought it would be good to dedicate a recipe to them, such as Angels on Horseback (totally inappropriate), or Quorn on the Cob! Instead he has chosen a recipe unique to the shires, the Stilton Tartlet. As many foxhunters munch their way through these, they will recall stirring gallops from the Stonepits via Clawson to Old Hills; a wonderful ride over big thorn fences and across the great green fields of the Belvoir Vale, from whence comes the 'King of Cheeses'.

To serve 4–6

125 ml/¼ pint [½ cup] double [heavy] cream
125 g/4 oz crumbled Stilton cheese
125 ml/¼ pint [½ cup] béchamel sauce
1 egg yolk
pinch of salt
¼ kg/½ lb shortcrust [pie] pastry

Roll out the shortcrust [pie] pastry and line a 18 cm/7 in. to 23 cm/9 in. pie dish; if there is any remaining pastry it can be made into a lid if desired.

Boil the double [heavy] cream until reduced by one third, stir in the béchamel sauce. Remove from the heat and stir in the egg yolk and crumbled Stilton. Add a little salt and allow the mixture to cool

When cool, spoon the mixture into the pie dish until about three-quarters full. Bake for 20 minutes in a pre-heated oven at 190°C/375°F/Gas Mark 5.

WOW-WOW SAUCE

A wonderful spicy sauce invented by an early nineteenth-century scientist and gourmet, Dr Kitchener. The odd name probably derived from the exclamation of the eater on trying the sauce for the first time. It is an excellent accompaniment for barbecues, steaks, grills and game, especially venison.

To serve 4–6

30 g/1 oz [¼ kg cup] plain [all purpose]
    flour
300 ml/½ pint [1¼ cups] strong stock
60 g/2 oz [4 tbsp] unsalted butter
1 tsp prepared English mustard
1 tbsp vinegar
1 tbsp tawny port
6 pickled walnuts, chopped
1 tbsp parsley, finely chopped

Melt the butter in a pan over a low heat, stir in the flour and cook for 2 to 3 minutes, stirring continuously. Slowly add the stock, stir well to get rid of any lumps. When the sauce is smooth and creamy, add the mustard, port and vinegar. Simmer and stir occasionally until it has a creamy consistency. Add the diced pickled walnuts and chopped parsley and cook for another minute or two. Serve at once with the game or meat.

MULBERRY AND APPLE JELLY

This spacious hostelry [The Fox and Hounds Hotel] was more like a continental inn than an English one; entered by a spacious archway from whose lofty ceilings hung the crooks, from whence used to dangle the glorious legs and loins of four-year-old mutton, the home-fed hams, the geese, the ducks, the game, with not unfrequently a haunch or two of presentation venison.

Ask Mamma, R. S. Surtees, 1858

This fruit jelly would make a marvellous accompaniment to any of the above mentioned meats whether hot roasted or cold.

To make approximately 8 lbs

granulated sugar, ½ kg/1 lb [2 cups] to
    each ½ litre/1 pint [2½ cups] fruit juice
1½ kg/3 lb mulberries
1 kg/2 lb cooking apples
1 litre/2 pints [5 cups] water
juice of 3 lemons

Wash the mulberries and put into a preserving pan. Roughly chop the apples (no need to core or peel) and add to the pan. Pour in the water and cook until the fruit is soft.

Put the fruit into a muslin bag or jelly bag. Hang up over-night to allow the juice to drip through into a bowl. Do not be tempted to squeeze the bag to quicken the process – if you do, the jelly will be cloudy.

When the juice has completely dripped through, measure, and to each ½ litre/1 pint [2½ cups] add ½ kg/1 lb [2 cups] granulated sugar. Put into a large saucepan, add the lemon juice and boil rapidly until setting point is reached. Test a little on a saucer to see if it will set.

Pour into warm, clean jars and seal in the usual way.

MARROW CHUTNEY

Mr Sponge having got two bountiful slices (of ham), with a knotch of home-made bread, and some mustard on his plate, now made for the table, and elbowed himself into a place between Mr Fossick and Sparks, immediately opposite Mr Spraggon.

Mr Sponge's Sporting Tour,
R. S. Surtees, 1853

This chutney would also have gone very well with the ham, as well as any cold and potted meats or cold game. Our friend Mr Sponge would have helped himself liberally had it been on Mr Springwheat's side board.

To make approx. 8–10 jars

1½ kg/3 lb vegetable marrow [large Zucchini], peeled and seeded
2 tsp salt
¼ kg/½ lb shallots, peeled and sliced
¼ kg/½ lb apples, peeled, cored and sliced
12 peppercorns
7½ g/¼ oz dried root ginger
¼ kg/½ lb [1½ cups] sultanas [golden raisins]
125 g/4 oz [½ cup] demerara sugar
¾ litre/1½ pints [3¾ cups] malt vinegar

Cut the marrow [large Zucchini] into small pieces, place in a bowl and sprinkle liberally with the salt, cover, and leave to stand for 1–2 hours. After this time, rinse and drain.

In a pan, put the marrow, shallots and apples. Tie the ginger and peppercorns in muslin and add to the pan along with the sultanas [golden raisins], vinegar and sugar. Bring to the boil then reduce the heat and simmer until the consistency is thick with no runny liquid in the mixture.

While the chutney is boiling, wash and heat your jam jars in the oven. When the chutney is ready, discard the muslin bag of spices and pour into the jars. Seal in the usual way and store.

A piece of material can also be secured around the lid of the jar with an elastic band; this looks attractive and the chutney could be used as a present.

AUTUMN FALL CHUTNEY

I love the fitful gust that shakes
The casement all the day,
And from the mossy elm tree takes
The faded leaves away,
Twirling them by the window pane
With thousand others down the lane.

The Shepherd's Calendar,
John Clare, 1827

This is an ideal chutney to use up any fruit that has been blown down by the exuberant autumn winds. Apples, pears, plums, all blend well together and are the perfect accompaniment to cold meat, game, cheese or pies.

To make approximately 4.5–5 kg/9–10 lb chutney

4 kg/8 lb any fruit, mixed or all of one
    variety
1 kg/2 lb onions, peeled and chopped
¼ kg/8 oz [1½ cups] mixed seedless raisins
    and sultanas [golden raisins]
1 kg/2 lb green tomatoes, washed and
    sliced
½ kg/1 lb vegetable marrow flesh, cut into
    small cubes
60 g/2 oz whole mixed pickling spice, tied
    in a muslin bag
¾ litre/1½ pints [4¾ cups] malt vinegar
¼ kg/8 oz [1 cup] soft brown sugar
60 g/2 oz salt

Cut away any bruised portions of fruit, peel and core where necessary. Chop into small chunks.

Put the fruit into a large, heavy-based pan. Add the tomato pieces, chopped onion, marrow flesh and the dried fruit. Put in the spices, pour in half the quantity of vinegar and bring to the boil, then simmer until tender and pulpy, stirring occasionally.

Put in the salt, sugar and the remaining vinegar, stir until the sugar has dissolved. Cook gently until the mixture becomes thick.

Remove the spice bag.

Pot and seal. Allow to mature for four to six weeks.

HORSERADISH SAUCE WITH LETTUCE HEARTS AND FRENCH DRESSING

Prior to the war, when playing an important polo match or competing in an International horse show, Sir Michael Ansell would enjoy rare, cold roast beef, and when playing polo at Hurlingham, his team would all have the same dish. After having eaten this, accompanied by this delicious salad, they were ready to take on any opposition.

For hundreds of years, the horseradish was used for medicinal purposes; grated with meat, it was thought to aid digestion. Sadly it is seldom seen in its raw state in the shops these days; however, if one is lucky enough to find any wild horseradish, the season in Britain is from September to the end of March.

2/3 tbsp grated horseradish, or creamed
    horseradish, depending on taste
2 tbsp lemon juice
pinch dry mustard
2 tbsp sugar
150 ml/¼ pint [½ cup] double [heavy]
    cream. This can be omitted if using
    one of the brands of creamed
    horseradish, though the addition of
    extra cream does enhance the texture
    and flavour.
2 lettuce hearts

Mix the lemon juice, grated or creamed horseradish, mustard, sugar, stir well together.

Whip the cream until it just holds its shape. Mix well and spoon over the lettuce hearts, or your roast beef.

THE BOWHILL SPECIAL

The first requisite for a grouse-shooter is patience; the next, a determination to make himself comfortable under any circumstances – and to put up with any inconveniences.

Thomas Oakleigh, 1837

These recipes were kindly supplied by The Duke of Buccleuch and Queensberry, K.T.

For each cup of hot Bovril add one measure of cheap port or sweet sherry and one measure of cheap brandy. Heat as usual and transport in thermos.

A variation of this is

THE DRUMLANRIG SPECIAL

Made as above, but substitute a double measure of whisky for the single measures of port and brandy. This is strongly recommended for cold shooting days, at almost any hour.

BLACK TREACLE SOUFFLÉ

Dark treacle or molasses is that which has had the most sugar removed from it. It was used as a sweetener in the north of England during the eighteenth century. Few people in the south could afford treacle as they were beset by the troubles caused by the Enclosures. This resulted in the people of the north gaining a reputation for inventing various dishes using treacle. Most recipes were for very substantial and filling puddings; this soufflé, however, is for modern palates, and though fairly rich, is not stodgy or too sweet.

To serve 6–8

175 g/6 oz [¾ cup] caster [superfine] sugar
6 large eggs, separated
5 tsp powdered gelatine [unflavoured gelatin]
5 tbsp cold water
425 ml/¾ pint [2 cups] double [heavy] or whipping cream
3 good tbsp black treacle [molasses], a little more if a stronger flavour is desired.

Prepare an 18 cm/7 in. soufflé dish by cutting a strip of greaseproof [wax] paper, long enough to go around the dish with the ends overlapping by about 7 cm/3 in. and deep enough to reach to the bottom of the dish and 9 cm/4 in. above the rim.

Tie the paper around the outside with string, fasten securely so that the string fits closely to the rim and prevents any of the mixture from escaping. The soufflé mixture is then poured into the dish to just above the rim, giving the appearance of having risen.

When the soufflé has set, remove the greaseproof [wax] paper carefully. Use a knife dipped into hot water and run it round the inside of the paper collar. It will come away quite easily.

Put the egg yolks and sugar into a large mixing bowl and whisk together. The mixture should become thick and mousse-like. Add the black treacle [molasses] and mix again until well blended.

Put the gelatine into a small cup or basin with the 5 tbsp of cold water and stand the basin in a saucepan of hot water and heat gently until the gelatine has dissolved. Allow to cool a little before adding to the soufflé mixture. Stir in gently and check that it is completely blended in.

Whisk 275 ml/½ pint [good cup] of the cream until it has the same consistency as the soufflé mixture. Stir into the soufflé mixture.

Whisk the egg whites until they just hold their shape (they must not be too dry or lumpy or they will not mix properly).

Fold the egg white very gently a third at a time into the soufflé. When evenly blended, pour into the prepared soufflé dish and chill for at least 4 hours.

When required, take away the greaseproof [wax] paper. Whisk the remaining cream and put into a piping bag with a star nozzle. Pipe cream rosettes onto the top of the soufflé. A small flower can be placed in the centre to give it a special, final touch.

MRS BEETON'S SOUFFLÉ OF CHOCOLATE

Sir, you are in snug quarters here. A sensible discreet person, your hostess, though a little gruff at the first brush, Sir, all good cooks are so. They know their own value – they are a privileged class – they toil in a fiery element – they lie under a heavy responsibility.

> Institution of the Cleikem Club,
> from *Cook and Housewife's Manual*,
> Mistress Margaret Dods, 1829

Anyone who has successfully cooked a hot soufflé will know the importance of good timing, and will also, like the lady mentioned above, know their own worth as a cook, and will be indeed in a privileged class. Mrs Beeton suggests that when cooked and ready to serve, the soufflé is wrapped around with a white napkin and sprinkled with vanilla sugar. It is a very handsome pudding to serve at a shooting lunch or hunt dinner.

To serve 4

4 large egg yolks
3 rounded tsp caster [superfine] sugar
125 g/4 oz plain dark [semisweet] chocolate, grated
4 egg whites, stiffly whisked
1 rounded tsp plain flour

Have ready a greased soufflé dish, and pre-heat the oven at 190°C/375°F/Gas Mark 5.

Beat the egg yolks, sugar, flour and grated chocolate together. When well blended, fold in the whisked egg white. Pour the mixture into the soufflé dish, and cook for 25–35 minutes. Serve at once with vanilla flavoured cream.

BREAD AND BUTTER PUDDING

From His Royal Highness,
The Prince of Wales

This ancient pudding has many variations, but the secret of its success lies in letting the pudding stand for an hour prior to baking, thereby allowing the bread to swell and absorb all the liquid, which makes it a light, crusty pudding. The addition of brandy turns the traditional nursery pudding into one a little more special. After we had tried this recipe, we saw why it is so favoured by His Royal Highness Prince Charles.

To serve 4

slices of buttered bread, enough to line a
    1 litre/2 pint oven-proof pie dish and
    for the topping
raisins, currants, sultanas [golden raisins],
    slices of banana, sufficient to the size
    of the dish
2 eggs
500 ml/1 pint [2½ cups] milk
brown sugar, according to taste
2 tbsp brandy
a little cinnamon to sprinkle on the top of
    the pudding
lots of cream for serving

Cut the buttered slices of bread into triangles. Grease the pie dish and arrange the bread in layers, sprinkling each layer with the fruit. Finish with a layer of bread, butter side up.

Beat the eggs and milk together, add the brandy. Sprinkle the sugar and cinnamon on top of the pudding and pour over the milk and brandy mixture. Allow to stand for about an hour, then bake for 30–40 minutes at 350°F/180°C/Gas Mark 4.

After this time, the pudding should be well risen with a golden crusty top. Serve hot with the cream.

BLACKBERRY AND APPLE PIE

While as the warm blaze cracks and
                  gleams
The supper reeks in savoury steams
Or kettle simmers merrily
And tinkling cups are set for tea
Thus doth the winter's dreary day
From morn to evening wear away.
         The Shepherd's Calendar,
             John Clare, 1827

After a cold day out in the open air this autumn fruit pie is something to look forward to. As the aroma pervades the kitchen, memory pictures those golden days when this black, shiny fruit clustered among the bramble hedges and apple trees hung green, red and russett from heavily laden branches. It is said that blackberries belong to the devil after 29 September, Michaelmas Day; it is therefore considered unlucky to pick the fruit after that day. Usually though, they are past their best, as an early frost can quickly spoil them. This sweet is a favourite with Derek Ricketts, which is not surprising after all the hard work and energy spent in the showjumping arena.

To serve 6

½ kg/1 lb blackberries, washed

1 kg/2 lb apples, peeled, cored and sliced
  (retain peel and cores)
225–255 g/7–8 oz [1 cup] sugar
255 g/8 oz shortcrust [pie] pastry to cover
  top of the pie

Sprinkle a little lemon juice over the apple
to prevent any discoloration.

Put half the quantity of blackberries
into a large saucepan. Put the apple peel
and cores into the pan with the fruit and
cover with water. Cook slowly at first
then increase the heat as the juices begin
to run. The cooking time will vary
according to the juice content of the fruit,
but it should be about 20 to 30 minutes.
Strain the liquid into a bowl and discard
the peel and cores.

Dissolve the sugar in the fruit juice;
the amount shown in the ingredients is
just a guide, and will depend upon
personal tastes.

Layer the apple slices and remaining
blackberries into a deep pie dish, pour
over the fruit juice and cover with the
shortcrust [pie] pastry. Brush the top with
egg white and sprinkle over a little caster
[superfine] sugar. Bake in the oven at
200°C/400°F/Gas Mark 6 for 15 minutes,
then turn down the temperature to 160°C/
325°F/Gas Mark 3, and cook for a further
45 minutes. If the pastry looks as though
it is turning too dark, cover with a piece
of kitchen foil. Test for cooking time by
inserting a knife into the apple; if it slips
through easily, then it is cooked. Serve
with clotted or double [heavy] cream or a
good home-made custard.

DARK CHOCOLATE PUDDING WITH HONEY AND WHISKY SAUCE

A great favourite with almost everyone
who loves puddings; it often appears on
the menu of shooting lunches during
autumn and winter.

To serve 4–6

30 g/1 oz [¼ cup] cocoa powder
125 g/4 oz [½ cup] butter or margarine
2 eggs, beaten
125 g/4 oz [½ cup] caster [superfine] sugar
a few drops of vanilla essence [extract]
a little milk to mix
180 g/6 oz [1½ cups] self-raising flour
  [cake flour plus 1 tsp baking powder]
For the sauce
1 wine glass of whisky
4 tbsp clear honey
¼ litre/½ pint [1¼ cups] milk
125 ml/¼ pint [½ cup] double [heavy]
  cream
juice of two lemons
1 heaped tbsp cornflour [cornstarch]

Half fill a large saucepan or steamer with
water and put it on to boil; grease a ¾
litre/1½ pint pudding basin.

Cream together the sugar and butter
or margarine until fluffy and pale. Add the
beaten egg and vanilla essence a little at a
time, beat well.

Make a smooth paste with the cocoa
powder by adding a tbsp of hot water.
Pour this into the egg mixture.

Sieve the flour and using a metal
spoon, fold in half the flour to the egg and
butter mixture. Add sufficient milk to give
a dropping consistency, fold in the
remaining flour and a little extra milk if

required to keep a smooth dropping texture. Pour the mixture into the basin, cover with greaseproof [wax] paper and secure with string. Steam for 1½ hours. To make the sauce, heat the ¼ litre/½ pint [1¼ cups] milk gently, slacken the cornflour [cornstarch] with a little cold water and add to the milk. Pour in the honey and stir well until the sauce thickens. Pour in the whisky and lemon juice, stir well. Gently beat in the cream.

Pour the sauce over the cooked hot pudding when ready to serve, or serve separately in a warm jug.

SPICED CRAB APPLES

Lo; Sweeten'd with the summer light,
The full juiced apple, waxing
over-mellow,
Drops in a silent autumn night.
Song of the Lotus Eaters,
Alfred, Lord Tennyson, 1832

Medieval cooks made sauces and pickles from verjuice, a kind of vinegar made from crab-apples. These spiced crab-apples may have been the forerunner of our familiar crab-apple jelly. Spiced apples are an unusual and excellent accompaniment to all game and cold meats.

To make 1 kg/2 lb

400 ml/¾ pint [2 cups] **malt vinegar (clear)**
1 kg/2 lb **crab apples**
½ kg/1 lb [2 cups] **brown sugar**
2 tsp **ground allspice**
2 tsp **ground cinnamon**

12 cloves and 1 piece of root ginger tied in a muslin bag

Remove the stalks and wash the apples. Prick them in a few places with a fork.

Pour the vinegar into a large heavy-based saucepan. Put in all the ingredients except the apples. Cook gently until the sugar has dissolved. Bring to the boil and simmer for 5 minutes.

Add the apples and simmer for a further 6–10 minutes until the apples are barely tender. Remove the apples with a slotted spoon and put them into warm, clean jars. The apples should be slightly firm to the touch.

Bring the liquid to the boil for about 30 minutes until reduced by half. Allow to cool so that it will not cook the apples when the liquid is poured into the jars.

Remove the muslin bag of spices and pour the liquid over the apples, filling the jars to the top. Cover and seal in the usual manner. Allow to mature for 8 weeks minimum.

RUM AND RAISIN CHEESECAKE

The record books tell us that cheesecakes were one of the earliest sweet puddings to be made, to use surplus milk from the dairy.

Many of today's recipes are American in origin, made from full fat soft cheese with a biscuit base. This recipe, however, is for a cooked cheesecake, and therefore it does not have a base. The combination of the two flavours give this sweet a festive air, but is obviously delicious at any time.

This is a very rich sweet, so it will serve about eight to ten people.

2 good tbsp dark rum
90 g/3 oz [¾ cup] raisins, soaked in the
    rum overnight to plump up the fruit
1 tsp vanilla essence [extract]
1 kg/2 lb cream cheese
125 ml/¼ pint [1¼ cups] double [heavy]
    cream
180 g/6 oz [¾ cup] caster [superfine] sugar
4 large eggs, lightly beaten
grated rind [zest] of 1 lemon
60 g/2 oz [½ cup] ground almonds
melted butter, sufficient to grease an
    20 cm/8 in. wide by 8 cm/3 in. deep
    cake tin (not a loose sided tin)

Pre-heat the oven to 170°C/325°F/Gas
    Mark 3

Brush the melted butter around the cake tin. Sprinkle the ground almonds around the sides of the tin; they should stick to the melted butter.

Put the cream cheese, sugar and cream into a blender and mix until smooth. Add the eggs, lemon rind [zest] and vanilla essence [extract], blend once more until well mixed together.

Pour the mixture into a bowl and fold in the soaked raisins evenly, add any rum that may be left in the soaking bowl. Pour the mixture into the prepared cake tin.

Cook the cheesecake by standing the tin in a pan of boiling water, the depth of which should come two-thirds up the side of the tin. Put into the pre-heated oven and cook for 2 hours until the cheesecake has a firm texture. Keep a check on the level of the water, top up if necessary.

When the cake is ready, turn off the heat, open the oven door and allow the cake to cool gradually, sitting in the oven.

When cool, turn out onto a plate. Serve with cream, fresh or sour.

CALEDONIAN CREAM

A sportsman noticed his gamekeeper attendant suffered from cold ears, so he purchased a pair of ear-muffs and gave them to the gamekeeper. Some weeks later while out on the moors the two men came together, and the sportsman noticed that the gillie did not wear the ear-muffs. 'What's the matter, Archie, where's your ear-muffs?'

'Weel sir,' replied the gamekeeper, 'one day a gentleman asked me to take a dram o' whisky an' I didna hear him, I've never worn them since.'

The Table in a Roar,
James Ferguson, 1933

To serve 4–6

30 g/1 oz [scant ¼ cup] caster [superfine] sugar
6 level tbsp thin shred marmalade (home-made if possible)
4 tbsp Drambuie
juice of 1 lemon
¼ litre/10 fl oz [1¼ cups] whipping or double cream

Mix together the marmalade, sugar, Drambuie and lemon juice. Whip the cream until the consistency reaches the soft peak stage. Gently fold the sugar and marmalade mixture into the cream. It can be whisked in, but care should be taken not to over-whip.

When well blended, serve in small glasses or bowls with a finger of shortbread.

MARMALADE WHISKY SAUCE

A very adaptable sauce that can be poured over pancakes, sponge puddings, milk puddings, ice-creams (served cold) and junkets. It is very simple to make and is a marvellous standby for those unexpected visitors.

To make sufficient for 4

3 rounded tbsp orange marmalade
3 tbsp white wine
3 tbsp whisky
2 level tbsp sugar (brown)
juice of ½ lemon

Gently heat the marmalade in a saucepan, add all the ingredients and simmer slowly for ten minutes. Pass through a sieve to be rid of any peel, pour into a jug and serve hot or cold.

THE QUAKER'S (GINGER) HUNTING NUTS

I began to perceive that I had been adopted as a pioneer by a small band of followers who, as one of their number candidly explained, 'I liked to have someone ahead of them to soften the bank,' and accordingly waited respectfully till the Quaker had made the rough places smooth, and taken the raw edges off the walls. They, in their turn, showed me alternative routes when the obstacle proved above the Quaker's limit.

Some Experiences of an Irish R.M.,
Somerville and Ross, 1899

A Day on the Hill
by Richard Ansdell.

Blowing for Cover, 1885,
by E.A.S. Douglas.

350 g/12 oz [1½ cups] unsalted butter
350 g/12 oz [1 cup] treacle
350 g/12 oz [1½ cups] caster [superfine] sugar
¼ kg/8 oz [1 cup] white flour
½ tsp bicarbonate of soda
360 g/12 oz medium oatmeal
3 tsp ground ginger

Melt the butter, treacle and sugar together in a saucepan, then add all the other ingredients, mix well together. When ready, roll the mixture into balls about the size of walnuts but a little flatter.

Bake in a moderate oven 180°C/350°F/Gas Mark 4, for 12–15 minutes.

MELTON HUNT CAKE

This cake is so named because it is as originally supplied to the members of the Melton Hunt, whose custom it was to eat a slice of the cake, together with a glass of sherry or 'stirrup cup', while mounted on horseback awaiting the start of the hunt. Dickinson & Morris Ltd have been making the cake at Melton Mowbray in Leicestershire, since 1854.

The original Melton Hunt Cake recipe has not changed since it was first made, but it does however remain a secret. Dickinson & Morris very kindly sent us a 'version' of the cake, to which we have made an addition or two, which hopefully keeps the delicious flavour and wholesomeness of the original recipe.

To serve 6–8

350 g/12 oz [2½ cups] currants
150 g/5 oz [1 cup] sultanas [golden raisins]
125 g/4 oz glacé cherries, cut in half

6 whole glacé cherries for decoration
90 g/3 oz blanched almonds, roughly chopped
12 whole almonds for decoration
grated rind [zest] of 1 small lemon
grated rind [zest] of 1 small orange
¼ kg/8 oz [2 cups] plain [all purpose] flour
1 tsp mixed spice
180 g/6 oz [¾ cup] best farmhouse butter, room temperature
3 large free-range eggs
1 port glass dark Jamaica rum
180 g/6 oz [¾ cup] soft brown sugar

Pre-heat the oven to 150°C/300°F/Gas Mark 1–2

Grease and line a 18 cm/7 in. round cake tin with silicone paper. Put the fruit and nuts into a bowl and pour in the rum. Leave to soak overnight.

Beat the butter and sugar together until soft and creamy. Beat in the eggs one at a time. Sift the flour and spice together.

Mix the grated rind [zest] of the orange and lemon into the butter and sugar mixture. Gradually add the fruit, nuts and flour stirring alternately into the butter and sugar. Pour in the remaining rum liquid. Mix well until all is smoothly blended together.

Mix in the chopped almonds and halved cherries, blend these in well also. Put the mixture into the cake tin. Lay the whole cherries and almonds on top and cook in the centre of the pre-heated oven for about 3 hours. When cooked, the cake should be moist.

After about 1¾ hours of cooking time, to prevent burning the nuts and cherries, cover the top of the cake with several thicknesses of greaseproof [wax] paper.

WINTER

The whole dinner, first, second, third, fourth course –
everything, in fact, except dessert – was on the table, as we
sometimes see at ordinaries and public dinners. Before both Mr
and Mrs Jorrocks were two great tureens of mock turtle soup,
each capable of holding a gallon, and both full up to the brim.
Then there were two sorts of fish : turbot and lobster sauce, and
a great salmon. A round of boiled beef, and an immense piece
of roast occupied the rear of these, ready to march on the
disappearance of the fish and soup – and behind the walls,
formed by the beef of Old England, came two dishes of grouse,
each dish holding three brace. The side dishes consisted of a
calf's head hashed, a leg of mutton, chickens, ducks, and
mountains of vegetables ; and round the windmill were plum-
puddings, tarts, jellies, pies and puffs.

Jorrocks's Jaunts and Jollities,
R. S. Surtees, 1838

MURPHY AND LEEK SOUP

'They took my sleeve to strain the soup,' repeated Philippa, in a crystal clarity of wrath. 'She said she got it in the press in the passage, ma'am, and she thought you were after throwin' it,' murmured Hannah, with a glance that implored my support.

'Who are you speaking of?' demanded Philippa, looking quite six feet high. The situation already sufficiently acute, was here intensified by the massive entry of Mrs Cadogan, bearing in her hand a plate, on which was a mound of soaked brownish rag. She was blowing hard, the glare of the kitchen range at highest power lived in her face.

'There's your sleeve ma'am,' she said, 'and if I could fall down dead this minute it'd be no more than a relief to me.'

Further Experiences of an Irish R.M.,
Somerville and Ross, 1908

To serve 6

2 large, 4 medium or 8 small potatoes,
    peeled and chopped
6 medium size leeks, cleaned and trimmed
750 ml/1½ pints [4 cups] hot milk
2 tsp salt
2 tbsp unsalted butter
125 ml/¼ pint [½ cup] single [light] cream
ground black pepper
1 tbsp chopped parsley

Chop the leeks into small pieces, melt the butter in a saucepan and sauté them until soft. Pour in 500 ml/1 pint [2½ cups] water and add the salt. Put in the chopped potato and cook for one hour, simmering gently, covered with a lid.

Pour in the heated milk, stir and liquidise until smooth. Season with the pepper, stir in the cream, heat very gently once more, taking care not to boil.

Serve sprinkled with the chopped parsley over each soup bowl.

VENISON AND MUSHROOM SOUP

A thaw, by all that is miserable; the gas lights mournfully reflect on the wet pavement, there is nothing to encourage the belief that there is a cab or coach to be had –. The cold sleet is drizzling down, the damp hangs upon the housetops and lamp-posts, and clings to you like an invisible cloak. The compound of ice, snow, and water on the pavement is a couple of inches thick.

Early Coaches from *Sketches by Boz*,
Charles Dickens, 1836–7

In the raw, dark, damp days of January, I rather think most of us would welcome this tasty, warming soup which is just right for lunch or supper with a chunk of home-made bread. The method for making this soup is quite involved, but it really is worth the extra time and effort.

To serve 4

For the stock
¾ kg/1½ lb stewing venison, plus any bones
    if you have them
2 leeks, washed and cut into inch thick
    rings
3 carrots, peeled and sliced

2 tbsp good dripping [beef fat] or bacon
    fat
1 stick celery, washed and chopped
2 onions, peeled and sliced
4 juniper berries, bruised
1 bay leaf
1 litre/2 pints [5 cups] water
½ litre/1 pint [2½ cups] red wine
For the soup
1 litre/2 pints [5 cups] of the venison stock
3 rashers [slices] smoked bacon, rind
    removed
1 onion, peeled and chopped
1 tbsp vegetable oil
90 g/3 oz button mushrooms
2 tsp blackberry jelly
1 sherry glass good port
salt and pepper
fried bread croutons for garnish

To make the stock, melt the fat in a large
stock pan. Chop up the venison and, a
little at a time, brown the meat in the fat.
A good brown colour is important for the
flavour of the soup.

When the meat is well browned, put
all the other ingredients into the pan,
bring to the boil, then simmer for 3–4
hours to extract all the goodness and
flavour of the meat and vegetables.

When ready, strain the liquid into a
bowl and allow to cool. When the fat has
set on the surface, remove and discard.
Any remaining meat and vegetables from
the stock can be discarded or maybe your
pet dog would welcome it in its meal.

The stock can be made a day or so in
advance of requirements.

To make the soup, put the oil into a
large saucepan and brown the onion.
Chop the bacon and add to the pan, cook
until crisp.

Wash and slice the mushrooms, put
them into the pan and cook until soft.

Add the port, blackberry jelly and the
stock, season well to taste and simmer for
45 minutes.

Serve in hot bowls with a few fried
bread croutons, a sprinkling of chopped
parsley and hot home-made bread.

117

SMOKY BACON AND LENTIL SOUP

I think most of us, at some time, have experienced the hard, bleak winters of northern Britain. What better welcome to come home to than this tasty, nourishing North Country soup, especially after a day's sport out on the snow covered moors and fells.

To serve 6–8

180 g/6 oz smoked streaky bacon, rind removed
250 g/8 oz [1¼ cups] lentils, soaked in cold water overnight
1 large leek, washed and chopped
2 large carrots, peeled and diced
2 large onions, peeled and chopped
2 sticks celery, washed and chopped
1 small swede, peeled and diced
1 bouquet garni
salt and black pepper
1½ litres/3 pints [7½ cups] chicken or vegetable stock

Chop the bacon and fry in a pan until just turning brown; a little fat can be added if desired. Remove the bacon and put to one side.

Fry the chopped onion in the bacon fat until just turning a pale brown, add the remainder of the diced and chopped vegetables and cook until all are slightly browned.

Drain the lentils, and put into a large saucepan along with the fried vegetables, onion and bacon. Pour in the stock and season well. Put in the bouquet garni or a handful of fresh herbs if you prefer. Bring to the boil, then simmer gently for 1½

hours. Remove any scum that may be on the surface.

When the lentils are cooked, remove from the heat, pour into a warmed soup tureen or soup plates. Decorate with more chopped, grilled [broiled] or fried bacon pieces, and a little chopped parsley sprinkled over.

OXTAIL SOUP

Oxtails have been used in cooking for centuries, only now it is the tail of the cow that is used, though retaining its old name.

Warming and nourishing, this soup is ideal for cold, wintery days, most welcome after any out-door pursuit.

To serve 4–6

1 oxtail, jointed. Any good butcher will do this, or they can be bought ready prepared
2 tbsp dripping [beef fat]
2 onions, peeled and chopped
2 carrots, peeled and chopped
3 sticks celery, washed and chopped
1 rasher [slice] bacon, rind removed
2 bay leaves
1½ litres/3 pints [7½ cups] stock
1 wine glass Hunting port, tawny port or dark sherry
salt and black pepper
bouquet garni
grated rind [zest] and juice of ½ lemon
2 tbsp plain [all purpose] flour

Heat the dripping [beef fat] in a large heavy frying pan or saucepan. Put in the oxtails and cook over a high heat, shaking the pan, until the meat is well browned on all sides. Remove the oxtail with a slotted spoon.

Add the chopped carrot, celery and onion. Chop the bacon then add this to the pan. Cook until golden brown, stir the vegetables to prevent sticking and burning.

Return the oxtails to the pan, add the stock, bay leaves, bouquet garni, salt and pepper. Bring to the boil, skim off any scum that may have risen to the surface, then simmer for 3 hours or until the meat is falling away from the bone.

After cooking time is completed, strain the stock into a large bowl and discard the vegetables, bay leaves and the bouquet garni. Allow the liquid to cool so that the fat rises to the surface and solidifies and it can be removed easily and discarded.

Take the meat from the bones, cut up any large pieces of meat. Discard the bones.

Heat a little more dripping [beef fat] in a saucepan and stir in the flour. Cook until the flour is well browned, add the stock and bring to the boil, stirring all the time until it is smooth and thick. Add the meat, lemon juice and rind [zest], simmer for a further 3 minutes, pour in the port or sherry, check the seasoning and serve with a large chunk of home-made bread hot from the oven.

GREEN PEA SOUP

'We twist up Chancery Lane, and cut along Holborn, and there we are in four minutes time, as near as a toucher. This is about a London Particular now, ain't it miss?' He seemed quite delighted with it on my account. 'The fog is very dense indeed' said I. 'Fog everywhere'.

Bleak House, Charles Dickens, 1852–3

The thick, brown-green London 'pea souper fogs', were a constant winter hazard. Charles Dickens describes the fog which gave its name to this soup because of its colour and thick consistency.

Unlike the fog, this soup is warm, nourishing and delicious. Ideal for those winter evenings after returning home cold, damp and hungry.

To serve 4–6

½ kg/1 lb dried peas, soaked overnight in cold water *or* ½ kg/1 lb fresh peas
4 rashers [slices] smoky bacon, rind removed and diced
2 carrots, peeled and diced
1 large onion, peeled and chopped
2 litres/4 pints [10 cups] vegetable or chicken stock
salt and black pepper
4 tbsp double [heavy] cream
2 tsp Worcestershire sauce
fried bread croutons

Put the diced bacon into a saucepan and cook gently until the fat begins to run. Add the chopped onion and carrot and cook until the fat has been absorbed.

Drain the soaked peas (if dried ones have been used) and put into the pan. Pour in the stock, season well, cover and simmer for 2 hours until the peas turn 'mushy'. Fresh peas should be cooked for 20 minutes.

Pass the cooked soup through a sieve or liquidise until smooth in a blender. Put the soup into a clean saucepan, add the Worcestershire sauce and double [heavy] cream. Re-heat to serve but do not boil.

Serve with a swirl of cream on top and a sprinkling of croutons.

BEEF BROTH WITH PARSLEY DUMPLINGS

What could be more welcoming to come home to than a bowl of hot broth, especially if laced with a drop of brandy or sherry. A good stock is most important as this will impart that wonderful flavour we associate with soups and broths, as well as the nourishing aspect of the ingredients.

To serve 6 good appetites

¼ kg/8 oz shin of beef
1 onion, peeled and chopped
1 stick celery, peeled and chopped
30 g/1 oz beef dripping [fat]
1 carrot, peeled and chopped
1 litre/2 pints [5 cups] good beef, chicken or vegetable stock
1 turnip, peeled and chopped
salt and black pepper
small glass brandy or sherry (optional)

For the dumplings
60 g/2 oz [¼ cup] shredded suet
1 tsp parsley chopped
125 g/4 oz [1 cup] self raising flour [cake
    flour plus ¾ tsp baking powder]
a pinch of salt

Cut the beef into cubes, melt the dripping
in a frying pan and fry the meat cubes
until nicely brown. Remove the meat and
put into the saucepan of stock.

Fry the vegetables in the dripping then
add these to the stock.

Put about one large spoon of stock
into the frying pan and stir round, to
collect the tasty meat juices. Scrape this
residue into the stock.

Season well, and simmer for 3 hours
minimum. The longer the broth simmers
the tastier it will be.

Make the dumplings by mixing all the
ingredients together with a little water.
Form into small dough balls and add to
the broth 25 minutes before completion of
cooking time.

A chunk of home-made, malted
wholemeal [whole wheat] bread is an
excellent accompaniment to make the
broth a meal in itself.

DEVILLED TROUT

Some, better pleased with private sport,
Use tennis; some a mistress court;
But these delights I neither wish
Nor envy, while I freely fish.

The Angler's Song,
Hugh Thomson and Austin Dobson, 1904

A marvellous dish for a cold winter's day;
hot, spicy and very easy to make. Tuna
fish or crab can be substituted for the trout
as all three make a very good first course
or a meal in itself.

To serve 6–8 as a first course

500 g/1 lb fresh trout meat, cooked and
    allowed to cool
180 g/6 oz [1½ cups] brown breadcrumbs
125 ml/¼ pint [½ cup] single [light] cream
1 large onion, finely chopped
90 g/3 oz [6 tbsp] unsalted butter
4 tsp Worcestershire sauce
4 tsp tomato purée [paste]
juice and grated rind [zest] of 1 lemon
1 tbsp anchovy essence [extract]
1 level tbsp curry paste per person – a little
    less if a milder flavour is required
grated Cheddar cheese for the topping

Melt the butter in a saucepan, add the
chopped onion and cook until soft.

Put the trout meat into a bowl, making
sure there are no bones. Add the cream,
onion, curry paste, breadcrumbs, lemon
juice and rind, tomato purée [paste],
Worcester sauce and anchovy essence
[extract].

Mix all the ingredients well until
thoroughly blended. Spoon the mixture
into ramekins or scallop shells, sprinkle
over a little grated cheese, pop a small
knob of butter on top of each ramekin and
grill [broil] until golden brown.

Decorate with a twist of lemon and a
sprig of fresh parsley.

PUPTON OF GAME

This way – this way – capital fun – lots of beer-hogsheads; rounds of beef-bullocks; mustard – cart-loads; glorious day – down with you – make yourself at home – glad to see you – very.

The Pickwick Club at the Cricket Match,
from *Pickwick Papers*,
Charles Dickens, 1837

To serve 4–6

8 pigeon or pheasant breasts
125 g/4 oz smoked streaky bacon, rinds
    removed and cut into pieces
4 shallots, peeled and sliced
90 g/3 oz mushrooms, washed and sliced
1 small leek, cleaned
160–175 ml/6 fl oz [¾ cup] red wine
sprig of fresh thyme
1 bay leaf
400 ml/¾ pint [2 cups] jellied beef or
    chicken stock
salt and black pepper

Put the pieces of bacon into a heavy-based saucepan and fry until the fat begins to run. Add the sliced shallots and cook until soft. Add the pheasant or pigeon breasts and sauté for ten minutes. Put in the sliced mushrooms.

Tie the leek, thyme sprig and bay leaf together with string and put this with the meat and onion. Pour in the red wine and 125 ml/¼ pint [good ½ cup] of the stock. Season well, and simmer gently for one hour.

Pour half the quantity of the remaining stock into a ring mould and put into the refrigerator to set.

When the meat is tender, remove the bundle of leek, thyme and bay leaf, discard. Put the pan ingredients along with the meat into a blender and liquidise until smooth. Place this meat mixture on top of the now set stock in the mould. Pour over the remaining stock and replace in the refrigerator to become very firm.

When required, dip the mould quickly into hot water and turn out the paté onto a serving dish.

Serve with hot buttered toast as a first course, or on triangles of toast or fried bread as a savoury.

ROAST BEEF AND YORKSHIRE PUDDING

A good honest fellow had a spare rib, on which he intended to sup with his family after a long and hard day's work at the coppice cutting. Home he came at dark, with his two little boys, each with a witch of wood that they had carried four miles, cheered with the thought of the repast that awaited them. In he went, and found his wife, the Methodist parson and a whole troup of the sisterhood, engaged in prayer, and on the table lay scattered the clean polished bones of the spare rib. . . .

Rural Rides,
William Cobbett, 1763–85

Roast beef has long been the traditional dish of England, even patriotic songs were written about it . . . 'O the roast beef of Old England, And O the Old English roast beef', is one national chorus. Having procured your beef, let us hope that it does not meet the same fate as that of the poor woodman's.

To serve 6–8

1 1½ kg/4 y lb roasting beef
2 tbsp dripping [beef fat]
For the Yorkshire pudding
2 large eggs
125 g/4 oz [1 cup] plain [all purpose] flour
250 ml/½ pint [1¼ cups] milk
good pinch of salt
For the gravy
250 ml/½ pint [1¼ cups] meat or vegetable
    stock
1 tbsp plain flour

Pre-heat the oven to 220°C/425°F/Gas
    Mark 7

Put the prepared beef joint into a roasting
tin with the dripping. Place in the oven for
15 minutes, then reduce the heat to 190°C/
375°F/Gas Mark 5 and roast for 15
minutes to ½ kg/1 lb if you like it rare, 20
minutes to ½ kg/1 lb if not.

To make the Yorkshire pudding, sieve
the flour and salt into a large bowl and
make a well in the centre. Break the eggs
into the well and add a little of the milk,
gradually draw in the flour using a
wooden spoon. Add a little more milk
gradually and mix well until you have a
thick batter. Beat until smooth, then stir in
any remaining milk. Leave to stand until
the meat is cooked.

When cooked, remove the beef from
the oven and keep warm. Increase the
oven temperature to 230°C/450°F/Gas
Mark 8. Cover the bottom of a baking tin
with a thin layer of fat from the meat
juices, and put into the oven until it is
smoking hot. Note that the baking tin
must not be too large, or the pudding will
not rise. Stir the batter mixture and mix

in two tablespoons of cold water, then
pour the batter into the baking tin. Bake
at the top of the oven for about 25 minutes
until well risen and a golden brown
colour.

Meanwhile make the gravy in the beef
roasting tin. Pour off as much fat as you
can whilst retaining the brown meat
juices. Mix the flour with the juices until
smooth, then add the stock, stirring all the
time. Put the tin over a low heat and stir
until the gravy thickens and boils. Pour
into a gravy boat and keep hot until
required.

When the pudding is ready, remove
from the oven and cut into squares; serve
as a first course with the gravy, as is
traditional in Yorkshire, or with the roast
beef. Any green vegetable can accompany
the beef, and of course, roast potatoes.

HUNTER'S CASSEROLE

Tain't the 'opping over 'edges as 'urts 'orses' 'oofs but the 'ammer, 'ammer, 'ammer on the 'ard 'igh road.

Jorrocks's Jaunts and Jollities,
R. S. Surtees, 1838

I think Mr Jorrocks would approve of this casserole after a ''ard days 'unting'. This dish can be made well in advance up to the French bread stage. It is a nourishing and warming meal.

To serve 6–8

1 kg/2 lb stewing or chuck steak, cut into small pieces
2 medium size onions, peeled and finely sliced
1 clove garlic, crushed with a little salt
$\frac{1}{4}$ litre/$\frac{1}{2}$ pint [1$\frac{1}{4}$ cups] beer
1 tsp red wine vinegar
French mustard to taste
3 tbsp dripping [beef fat]
1 tbsp plain flour
125 g/4 oz lean gammon or ham, cut into small pieces
1 level tbsp brown sugar
salt and pepper
1 tsp thyme, chopped
slices of French bread, sufficient to cover the top of the casserole

Put half the amount of dripping [beef fat] into a large frying pan and fry the slices of onion until they are just turning brown, remove from the pan and put to one side.

Add the remainder of the dripping and brown the beef pieces, remove and put to one side.

Put into the pan the gammon or ham and seal quickly for a few moments, remove, and put with the beef.

Put the flour into the pan and stir well, then add the crushed garlic. Return the onion to the pan and stir well together, pour in the beer and vinegar, add the sugar and bring to the boil. Remove the pan from the heat.

Put the meat into an oven-proof dish, pour over the liquid, season well, sprinkle over the chopped thyme. Add a little water, enough to just cover the meat, cover, and cook in a slow oven for 2 to 2$\frac{1}{2}$ hours.

Just before the cooking time is up, spread the French mustard onto the slices of French bread, put the bread on top of the casserole, and finish cooking with the lid removed.

PORK FILLET WITH A CIDER AND APPLE SAUCE

Well can we recall the monster hearth and fire at Farnborough, where, at first, unable to find our fingers to unbutton our coats, we broke in, half frozen. . . .

The Coaching Age,
Stanley Harris, 1885

There are not many sportsmen and women who have escaped the experience of feeling half frozen and wet through after a day in open country. This dish would be very welcome whether it be sporting guests, travellers, or a few invited friends to dinner. Well-seasoned creamed potatoes and Brussels sprouts are an excellent accompaniment.

To serve 4

2 pork tenderloins [fillets]
1 onion, peeled and finely chopped
2 eating apples, peeled, cored and sliced
juice of ½ lemon
3 tbsp vegetable oil
3 tbsp double [heavy] cream
150 ml/¼ pint [½ cup] sweet cider
90 g/3 oz [6 tbsp] unsalted butter
salt and black pepper

Cut each pork fillet into 4 pieces and lay them on a board, cover with cling film [wrap], and with a rolling pin, beat flat.

Put 30 g/1 oz [2 tbsp] of the butter into a pan, add the onion, and cook until soft. Add the apple slices and cook gently, mixing the apple and onion together and remove from the pan, put to one side.

Add the remaining butter and the oil to the pan, put in the pork pieces, and sauté until the meat is tender, turning the pieces from time to time. When the pork is cooked, remove from the pan and keep warm.

Return the apple and onion to the pan, pour in the cider and lemon juice, simmer until the liquid is slightly reduced and the apple cooked through. Pour in the cream, season well to taste. Stir all the ingredients round the pan, do not boil at this stage.

Arrange the pork fillets on a warm serving dish and pour the sauce over the meat. Sprinkle with chopped parsley and a few more slices of apple if desired. Serve at once.

QUORN BACON ROLL

The Quorn Hunt gave its name to this nourishing dish which was traditionally given to the hunt servants.

To serve 6–8

¼ kg/8 oz [1 cup] shredded suet
1 tsp salt
½ kg/1 lb [4 cups] self-raising flour [cake flour plus 3 tsp baking powder]
1 tbsp chopped parsley, fresh
For the filling
½ kg/1 lb bacon rashers [slices], rinds removed
2 medium onions, peeled and chopped
2 tsp made English mustard
salt and ground black pepper
2 tsp fresh sage, chopped

Sift the flour and salt together into a bowl. Add the suet and pour in sufficient water to form into a firm dough.

Roll out on a floured board into a rectangle 1 cm/½ in thick. Lay the bacon rashers [slices] on top of the pastry, spread the mustard onto the bacon, sprinkle over the chopped onion and sage. Season well.

Roll up as for a Swiss roll [jellyroll] and wrap in a sheet of kitchen foil, fold and crimp the edges to seal.

Place in a steamer over a pan of boiling water and cook for 2½ hours. Top the pan up with more boiling water when necessary.

Remove the wrapping and put the roll onto a warm dish. Sprinkle over the chopped parsley and serve with lots of tasty gravy and vegetables.

KIDNEYS IN A FRESH ORANGE AND RAISIN SAUCE

There had been a sharp frost for some time, and no hunting to be had, and sporting undergraduates were at their wits' end what to do – some, indeed, did not scruple to say that if the weather did not change they should take to reading!

> Christ Church, Oxford, 1819,
> from *Sporting Days & Sporting Ways*,
> Ralph Nevill

Maybe those unfortunate undergraduates should have given a dinner with this dish as an excellent starter. It would have been a lot less trouble than the antics those bored students got up to, such as putting a leaden statue of Mercury, which stood in the college's quadrangle into the fountain – no easy task.

To serve 4

8 lambs' kidneys, washed, skinned and cut in half to remove cores
90 g/3 oz [6 tbsp] unsalted butter
1 onion, peeled and finely chopped
1 clove garlic, crushed with a little salt
60 g/2 oz [scant ½ cup] raisins soaked in 100 ml/4 fl oz [½ cup] port or red wine
100 ml/4 fl oz [½ cup] stock
2 level tbsp seasoned flour
juice and grated rind [zest] of 1 large orange
2 tsp redcurrant jelly
chopped parsley for decoration

Toss the prepared kidneys in the seasoned flour. Melt the butter in a saucepan and sauté the kidneys for 2 to 3 minutes. Add the onion and garlic and cook for a further 5 minutes.

Gradually pour in the stock, wine and raisins, juice and rind [zest] of the orange. Season well and simmer gently for ten minutes until the kidneys are tender.

Remove the kidneys and boil the sauce rapidly. Add the redcurrant jelly, stir well to dissolve the jelly.

Pour the sauce over the kidneys and sprinkle with the chopped parsley.

The kidneys can be served with boiled rice or creamed potatoes as a main course.

ESCALOPES [SCALLOPINE] OF TURKEY WITH A HAZELNUT CREAM SAUCE

It was late in the afternoon when the four friends and their four footed companion turned into the lane leading to Manor Farm; 'Why, where have you been?' said the hospitable old gentleman [Mr Wardle]. 'I've been waiting for you all day. Well you do look tired. What: scratches; Not hurt, I hope – eh? So you've been spilt, eh? Never mind. Common accidents in these parts. We'll have you put to rights here,' said the old gentleman, 'and then I'll introduce you to the people in the parlour. Emma, bring out the cherry brandy.'

> Mr Pickwick Drives,
> from *Pickwick Papers*,
> Charles Dickens, 1837

A dish such as this one would be most welcome after being run away with and spilt by your carriage horse. It is to be hoped that escapades like that are few, but the occasions to enjoy this delicious main course are many. Chicken breasts, and pork tenderloin can be used instead of the turkey if preferred.

It is a very quick and easy dish to prepare, especially when served with a green salad and buttered pasta, though of course the usual vegetables will make it a more substantial meal.

To serve 4

½ kg/1 lb fresh turkey escalopes [scallopine]
5 tbsp good medium sherry
5 tbsp double [heavy] cream
90 g/3 oz [6 tbsp] **unsalted butter**
60 g/2 oz **hazelnuts, finely chopped**
salt and black pepper
paprika to garnish

Beat the escalopes [scallopine] between two pieces of greaseproof [wax] paper.

Melt the butter in a frying pan and sauté the escalopes for 4 to 5 minutes, turning once. Remove from the pan to a warm place.

Reduce the heat and stir in the cream and sherry, season well, add the hazelnuts and cook for 1 minute. Pour the sauce over the turkey, sprinkle with paprika and serve.

DUCK WITH FRESH ORANGE

Maria's performance was faultless; in half a minute she had laid a bird at my feet, a very large pale drake, quite unlike any wild drake that I had ever — : Out of the silence that followed came a thin, shrill voice from the hill: 'Thim's Mrs Brickley's ducks.'

In horrid confirmation of this appalling statement I perceived the survivors already landing on the far side of the lake, and hurrying home-ward up the hill with direful clamours, while a wedge shaped ripple in the grey water with a white speck at its apex, told of Minx in an ecstasy of pursuit!

Further Experiences of an Irish R.M.,
Somerville and Ross, 1908

Wild duck is much richer in flavour than the domestic variety. Mallard, teal and widgeon are the types of wild duck most likely to grace the dining table. Duck is usually hung for from two to three days and care should be taken not to over-cook or the bird will become quite tough. The fruitiness of the orange marries well with the rich tasting meat and is especially good when accompanied by a bottle of good beaujolais or a fruity burgundy.

This dish is one of Harvey Smith's favourite and no doubt very much relished after a hard day's show-jumping or out in the hunting field.

To serve 4–6 depending on appetites and duck size

2 duck, totalling 2–2½ kg/4–5 lbs,
    prepared for roasting
100 ml/4 fl oz [½ cup] red wine vinegar
4 oranges
juice of ½ lemon
1 level tbsp arrowroot
1 level tbsp caster [superfine] sugar
300 ml/10 fl oz [1¼ cups] giblet stock or
    any good strong stock
3 tbsp Grand Marnier

Pre-heat the oven to 200°C/400°F/Gas Mark 6

Peel the oranges over a bowl to catch the juice, remove the pith and divide the fruit flesh into segments. Cut the rind [zest] into strips and boil them for ten minutes in a little water, drain, and set aside with the segments for the garnish.

Grease a roasting tin and place the prepared ducks on their sides in the tin. Put into the oven and cook for 40 minutes, then turn the ducks over onto their other side and cook for 30 minutes, then turn the ducks once more, this time onto their backs and cook for a further 30 minutes. Baste frequently throughout cooking times.

Boil the vinegar and sugar together until reduced to a light caramel. Add the orange and lemon juice, pour in the stock and boil for five minutes. Dilute the arrowroot in a little cold water then pour into the sauce, stir well until thick and shiny. Strain the sauce and add the Grand Marnier.

When the ducks are ready, place them on a warm serving dish and pour over the sauce. Top with the strips of orange peel and the segments, sprinkle over a little chopped parsley and serve with an orange and green salad, peas, and if in season new potatoes; if not in season, sautéed or croquet potatoes.

The Barraud Brothers out Shooting, 1831,
by William Barraud.

The Sportsmen, 1885,
by Thomas Byron Lyle.

HASHED ROAST DUCK WITH PORT

And behold, on the first floor, at the court-end of the house, in a room with all the window-curtains drawn, a fire piled half-way up the chimney, plates warming before it, wax candles gleaming everywhere, and a table spread for three, with silver and glass enough for thirty –

A famous Inn,
from *Martin Chuzzlewit*,
Charles Dickens, 1843–4

This is a very tasty way to use up any left over duck, or indeed any game bird. A good dish to serve at a shooting lunch or supper to warm up cold and possibly wet hunters.

To serve 4

¼ kg/1 lb cold roast duck
700 ml/1¼ pint [3 cups] good game or beef
    stock
1 onion, peeled and sliced
60 g/2 oz [4 tbsp] butter
60 g/2 oz [½ cup] flour
salt and cayenne pepper
¼ tsp minced lemon peel [zest]
juice of ½ lemon
2 port glasses good port
30 g/1 oz [2 tbsp] unsalted butter
chopped parsley to garnish

Dice the duck meat and reserve the trimmings.

Melt the unsalted butter in a pan and lightly fry the onion. Add the trimmings, stir, then pour in the stock. Simmer gently for 1 hour. Strain the liquid into another saucepan, discard the trimmings.

In a separate pan melt the butter and stir in the flour, cook until you have a pale brown roux. Pour in the stock liquid and beat in the roux thoroughly. Season to taste with the salt and cayenne pepper.

Pour in the port, lemon juice and rind [zest]. Bring to the boil and skim off any fat. Put in the diced duck meat and heat gently for ½ hour. Place in a serving dish, sprinkle over the chopped parsley and if desired a handful of fried bread croutons.

Serve with creamed potatoes, well seasoned, and any other fresh vegetable.

ROAST GOOSE WITH A QUINCE, PRUNE AND APPLE STUFFING

There never was such a goose. Bob said he didn't believe there ever was such a goose cooked. Its tenderness and flavour, size and cheapness, were the themes of universal admiration. Eked out by apple sauce and mashed potatoes, it was a sufficient dinner for the whole family.

A Christmas Carol,
Charles Dickens, 1843

To serve 8

1 goose around 5 kg/10 lb, plucked and
    oven ready
½ kg/1 lb apples, peeled, cored and
    chopped
¼ kg/½ lb quince, peeled, cored and
    chopped
¼ kg/½ lb prunes, soaked overnight, stoned
    and chopped
2 fresh sage leaves finely chopped
2 level tbsp soft brown sugar
¼ litre/½ pint [1¼ cups] chicken stock
¼ litre/½ pint [1¼ cups] medium cider
2 tbsp crab apple or redcurrant jelly
salt and black pepper

Wipe the goose inside with kitchen paper and prick the skin all over with a fork to allow the fat to come away. Rub the goose all over with the salt and pepper.

Mix together the apples, quince, prunes, sage and brown sugar. Fill the inside of the goose with the fruit and secure with a skewer.

Stand the bird on a wire rack in a roasting tin and cook in a pre-heated oven 190°C/375°F/Gas Mark 5 for 3½ to 4 hours. To check if the goose is cooked,

prick the thickest part of the leg with a knife; if the juices do not run pink, it is ready.

When the goose is ready, place onto a serving dish and keep warm. Remove the fat from the roasting juices and pour in the cider. Stir well to incorporate the goose juices.

Pour the liquid into a saucepan and add the stock, boil rapidly for about 15 minutes. Stir in the crab apple or redcurrant jelly. If desired the gravy can be thickened with 1 tbsp of cornflour [cornstarch] mixed with 4 tbsp of water.

Pour the gravy into a warm sauce boat and serve the goose with peppered creamed potatoes, Brussels sprouts and apple sauce.

SALMI OF SNIPE

Eventually we did get a few snipe, and then we returned to the farm house – where we found a sumptuous tea laid out and a bottle of whisky on the table. After we and our host had 'wished' each other good luck, we were left to have our tea. My companion immediately proceeded to pour half the bottle of whisky out of the window, in spite of my protests that it was a shame to waste the good man's liquor. He said that if we didn't we should have the whole bottle to finish. Presently our host returned to see how we were getting on, and was most disappointed with how we were getting on with the whisky. My companion proved quite right: out of that house we did not get till the bottle was empty. . . .

English Sport,
Captain H. F. R. Hardy, 1932

This dish is ideal for a light lunch or supper dish or served as a first course. Crisply fried bread and a fresh salad are an excellent accompaniment.

To serve 4

4 oven ready snipe
2 onions, peeled and finely chopped
4 rashers [slices] smokey bacon, rind
    removed
2 tsp redcurrant jelly
$\frac{1}{2}$ tsp cayenne pepper
sprig of lemon thyme
125 ml/$\frac{1}{4}$ pint [$\frac{1}{2}$ cup] white stock
8 tbsp Burgundy wine
salt and black pepper
juice and grated rind [zest] of $\frac{1}{2}$ lemon
twists of lemon for garnishing

Pre-heat the oven to 220°C/425°F/Gas
    Mark 7

Secure a bacon rasher [slice] around each snipe. Put the birds into an oven-proof dish and roast in the pre-heated oven for 15 minutes. Remove from the oven after this time (the snipe should still be under-cooked).

Remove the bacon and lay onto a grill pan to crispen for the garnish.

Cut each snipe into four joints, two legs and two breasts. Put the meat joints into a saucepan. Pour in the stock, add the cayenne pepper, wine, onion pieces, lemon juice and rind [zest], sprig of thyme, redcurrant jelly, salt and pepper to taste. Simmer for 20 minutes over a gentle heat.

Remove the thyme sprig and serve the snipe on pieces of fried bread with the sauce poured over or served separately. Garnish with the twists of lemon slices, sprinkle over the crispy crumbled bacon.

ROAST PARTRIDGE WITH A PEAR SAUCE

Out of the dawn had a light snow drifted,
The line of the road was limned in white,
And over the edge of the world it lifted
Beautiful, burnished, broad and bright.
The Golden Hoofprints
from *Galloping Shoes*,
Will H. Ogilvie, 1922

A very good dish for a shooting lunch or dinner party. It is easy to prepare, and when decorated with fresh pear slices, bunches of watercress, and fried breadcrumbs, it is a very appealing dish visually as well as an appetizing one.

To serve 4

4 partridge, plucked, cleaned and ready for the oven
1 small clove garlic, crushed with a little salt
8 rashers [slices] of smoked streaky bacon
5 just ripe pears (not too ripe or they will lose their flavour in cooking)
2 tsp sugar
125 ml/¼ pint [½ cup] dry vermouth
4 tbsp single [light] cream
couple of bunches of watercress for decoration
fried breadcrumbs
game chips (or potato crisps [chips] if time is at a premium)
salt and black pepper

Rub each partridge with the crushed garlic. Wrap each bird with two rashers [slices] of bacon and roast in the oven for 10 minutes at 225°C/450°F/Gas Mark 8.
Then reduce the heat to 200°C/400°F/ Gas Mark 6, and cook for a further 20 to 30 minutes depending on size of partridge. Remove after they are cooked, put onto a serving dish and keep warm.

De-glaze the roasting pan by adding the dry vermouth to the meat juices in the pan, stir round well then pour into a saucepan and season well. Peel and core 4 of the pears, cut into slices and put into the saucepan.

Cook gently for a couple of minutes, then put the sauce into a blender with the sugar and single [light] cream. Blend quickly together then re-heat but do not boil. Pour the sauce into a sauce boat and keep warm.

Peel, core and slice the remaining pear and arrange around the edge of the serving dish. Arrange the watercress around the partridge, and serve with the hot breadcrumbs and game chips.

If you wish, the bacon can be chopped roughly and either sprinkled over the birds or sprinkled into the sauce.

BREAST OF PHEASANT IN A CHESTNUT SAUCE

There's a thrill in the thunder of
galloping horses
As they race o'er the turf of
England's courses.
Here they come, can you see
the silken bands
Of the hot blooded riders flash by
the stands?

Here comes Eclipse, sixteen hands tall,
Where are the rest–? Nowhere at all.
There's a thrill in the speed of
                    this equine host
As greased lightning he passes
                the winning post.
Galloping Horses,
Nikki Rowan-Kedge, 1989

After a day at the races, especially if you
have had a winner or even more than one,
what better way to celebrate than by
having this dish as a special main course?
Even better, it can be prepared in advance,
so it can be heated up when required. Well
seasoned creamed potatoes and buttered
carrots are an excellent accompaniment.

To serve 4

4 pheasant breasts
1 tin natural chestnuts
6 shallots, peeled and chopped
$\frac{1}{4}$ litre/$\frac{1}{2}$ pint [1$\frac{1}{4}$ cups] beef or game stock
1 small wine glass fruity white wine
4 tbsp double [heavy] cream
2 tsp redcurrant jelly
1 tsp fresh chopped tarragon
2 tsp fresh chopped parsley
60 g/2 oz [$\frac{1}{2}$ stick] unsalted butter
1 tbsp vegetable oil
1 large clove garlic, crushed with a little
    salt

Melt the oil and butter in a large pan, add
the chopped shallots and cook until just
turning brown. Remove the shallots and
put to one side.

Put the pheasant breasts into the pan
and cook on both sides until golden
brown; this seals in the juices.

Put in the crushed garlic, wine, the
cooked shallots, stock and chestnuts. Stir
well then add the herbs, season well and
simmer gently until the pheasant is tender,
around 15 to 20 minutes, though this will
depend on the age of the bird. The older
the pheasant the longer the cooking time.

When the meat has cooked, remove
from the pan and keep warm. Boil the
sauce rapidly until reduced by a quarter.
Put the sauce into a blender and liquidise
until smooth and creamy. Add the cream
and redcurrant jelly. If the sauce is too
thick for your taste, add a little water to
slacken.

Pour the completed sauce over the
pheasant breasts and serve, or put into a
container to keep until required.

SLOE ROASTED PHEASANT

If a sportsman true you'd be,
Listen carefully to me.
Keep your place and silent be:
Game can hear and game can see;
Don't be greedy, better spared
Is a pheasant than one shared.
A Father's Advice to His Son,
Mark Beaufoy

This slightly unusual sauce, made from
sloe gin, accompanies and blends perfectly
with the normal roast pheasant. It gives
the meat a slightly piquant flavour and the
sauce itself is delicious. Homemade sloe
gin is best, but if you do not have any
made, Gordon's make an excellent brew.

To serve 4

brace of pheasant, plucked and oven ready
12 juniper berries
2 tsp redcurrant jelly
125 ml/¼ pint [½ cup] sloe gin
125 ml/¼ pint [½ cup] water
4 rashers [slices] streaky bacon
4 slices of bread cut to shape for frying
salt and black pepper

Place 6 juniper berries inside each
pheasant, wrap the bacon around the
birds and put into a hot oven 230°C/
450°F/Gas Mark 8. Cook for 25 minutes
then lower the temperature to 190°C/
375°F/Gas Mark 5. Cook for a further 25
to 30 minutes, depending on size of birds.
Mix the gin with the water and baste the
pheasants from time to time during
cooking. The cooking time may take a
little longer if heat loss has occurred
during basting.

About 10 to 15 minutes before cooking
time is completed, remove the bacon to
allow the breast meat to brown.

When the pheasant is completely
cooked, remove from the oven, carve the
meat and arrange on a warm serving dish.
Keep hot.

Stir the juices from the roasting tin,
mixing in the meat juices. Add any sloe
gin and water left over from the basting.
Add the redcurrant jelly. Season well and
simmer gently for a couple of minutes.

The sauce is ready to serve if you like
a thin sauce; if a thicker one is required,
add three tsp of cornflour [cornstarch]
slackened with a little water.

Fry the bread slices and put with the
pheasant. Pour the sauce into a sauce boat
or over the pheasant. Decorate with sprigs
of fresh watercress and/or parsley.

HASHED PHEASANT

At the dinner-table the Rector glowed
with austere geniality while he carved the
brace of pheasants which represented a
days covert-shooting he'd had with Lord
Dumborough.

Memoirs of a Fox-Hunting Man,
Siegfried Sassoon, 1928

This is an excellent way to use up any left
over pheasant or venison. The secret of
success is in the quality of the gravy and
claret. Serve with creamed potatoes and
pureé of carrot and swede.

To serve 4

½ kg/1 lb cold, cooked pheasant cut into
 bite-sized pieces
½ litre/1 pint [2½ cups] good brown stock
 or gravy
1 wine glass good red wine or claret
salt and black pepper
1 tbsp redcurrant jelly or dark marmalade
1 small clove garlic crushed with a little
 salt
60 g/2 oz [4 tbsp] unsalted butter or 2 tbsp
 vegetable oil

Melt the butter or oil in a saucepan and
cook the crushed garlic. Put the meat into
the pan and toss and stir quickly.

Pour in the stock or gravy and the
wine, season well and simmer gently for
15 to 20 minutes.

Add the redcurrant jelly or marmalade
and cook for a further 10 minutes, stirring
well.

Check the seasonings, put into a dish
and serve hot. A few fried bread croutons
can be scattered over the dish if desired.

ROAST WOODCOCK

That frosty evening was followed by three
others like unto it, and a flight of
woodcock came in. I calculated that I
could do with five guns, and I dispatched
invitations to shoot and dine on the
following day to four of the local
sportsmen, among whom was, of course,
my landlord.

Some Experiences of an Irish R.M.,
Somerville and Ross, 1899

1 woodcock per person, prepared by your
 game dealer
white bread
brown breadcrumbs
melted unsalted butter
salt and pepper
2 rashers [slices] of streaky bacon per bird

Pre-heat the oven to 200°C/400°F/Gas
 Mark 6

Brush each bird with melted butter and
place it on a piece of thick white bread,
crusts removed. Lay over the bacon
rashers [slices] and season well. Roast in
the hot oven for 15 minutes.

Fry the breadcrumbs in melted butter
and serve with the roast woodcock,
accompanied by bread sauce, sautéed
potatoes and green vegetables.

SADDLE OF HARE WITH A
BLACKBERRY SAUCE

'I mean 'are-'unting; it is a werry nice
ladylike amusement; and though we have
had no 'are soup at dinner, I make no
doubt we have some werry keen 'are-
'unters at table for all that. I beg to give
you '''are-'unting and the merry Dotfield
'Arriers''.'

Handley Cross,
R. S. Surtees, 1843

This dish needs a couple of days advance
preparation, as the hare needs to be well
marinaded. The finished product will be
worth the effort.

To serve 4

saddle of young hare
1 clove garlic crushed with a little salt
2 tbsp soft dripping [beef fat] or bacon fat
For the marinade
$\frac{1}{2}$ litre/1 pint [$2\frac{1}{2}$ cups] medium cider
5 tbsp raspberry vinegar
large fresh sprig of parsley and thyme
1 bay leaf
1 small onion, peeled and thinly sliced
For the sauce
1 small wine glass brandy
$\frac{1}{2}$ kg/1 lb fresh or frozen blackberries
4 tsp blackberry or redcurrant jelly
125 ml/$\frac{1}{4}$ pint [$\frac{1}{2}$ cup] single [light] cream

Rub the prepared saddle of hare with the
crushed garlic. Put the marinade
ingredients into a large container, immerse
the hare in the liquid and leave for two
days in a cool place.

After two days remove the hare from
the marinade, dry the meat with kitchen

paper and place in a roasting tin.

Strain the marinade liquid into a bowl
and reserve for basting.

Rub the hare with the dripping or
bacon fat, then put into a very hot oven
230°C/450°F/Gas Mark 8 for 50 minutes,
basting often with the marinade liquid.

When cooked and tender remove the
hare from the oven, put onto a serving
dish and keep warm. Remove any fat from
the roasting juices and pour the juices and
the remaining marinade liquid into a
saucepan. Add the blackberry or
redcurrant jelly and brandy and boil
rapidly to reduce the liquid slightly. (If a
thicker sauce is desired, now add 2 level
tsp cornflour [cornstarch] slackened with
four tbsp of water.)

Remove from the heat and stir in the
cream and three quarters of the
blackberries. Pour the completed sauce
into a warm sauce boat and decorate the
saddle of hare with the remaining
blackberries and sprigs of fresh parsley.

JUGGED HARE

Gaunt greyhounds now their coursing
                                    sports impart –
Wi' long legs stretched on tip toe for
                                    the chase
And short loose ear and eye upon the start
Swift as the wind their motions
                                    they unlace
When bobs the hare up from her
                                    hiding place
Who in its furry coat of fallow stain
Squats on the lands or wi a dodging pace
Tryes its old coverts of wood grass to gain
And oft by cunning ways makes
                            all their speed in vain
                                    The Shepherd's Calendar,
                                        John Clare, 1827

Hare stewed in its own juices and enriched
with wine and herbs, is a marvellous dish
to fortify anyone after a busy day in the
open air. Served with peppered, creamed
potatoes and green vegetables a dish such
as this would make most people feel
replete.

To serve 4

1 hare, skinned, cleaned, jointed and
    dressed
beef stock, enough to cover the hare in the
    casserole
2 medium sized onions, peeled and sliced
juice of $\frac{1}{2}$ lemon
salt and black pepper
a few cloves
oil and unsalted butter in equal quantities
    to fry the hare
1 good tbsp redcurrant jelly
large glass good red wine
$\frac{1}{4}$ tsp grated nutmeg
2 tsp fresh parsley, chopped

Fry the joints of hare in the butter and oil
to seal in the juices. Place the meat into a
casserole along with the beef stock, onion,
lemon juice, cloves, nutmeg, parsley, salt
and pepper. Cook in the oven until the
meat is tender, 170°C/325°F/Gas Mark 3
for 3–4 hours. Allow to cool.

When cool, discard the cloves, remove
the meat from the bones and return the
meat to the casserole. Add the red wine
and redcurrant jelly. Re-heat the casserole,
adjust the seasoning if desired.

Thicken the gravy by removing the
meat and boiling the liquid until reduced
by half. Replace the meat and serve with
the suggested vegetables and a chunk of
home-made wholemeal [whole wheat]
bread.

BAKED FISH POT

This old country dish was made of any damaged, broken fish that was no use for market, or any odd fishes left over in the packing sheds. It was by custom given away at the quayside, but some old 'fishwomen' would sell it from barrows in the street. The fish was often not sold by weight but by measure, using a small wooden board about a foot long by six inches wide and laying the strangely assorted fish out along the board – in a ragged row – long and short, thin and fat, side by side. 'A shilling a boardful, missus; Hall frush fussh.'

Food in England,
Dorothy Hartley, 1954

To get the fullest flavour it is important that a good quality dripping [beef fat] and large well flavoured onions are used, together with an oven-proof pot with a well fitting lid which allows the fish to steam in its own juice.

To serve 4–6

2–4 fish depending on size, i.e. sole, whiting, cod
2 large onions, peeled and chopped
180 g/6 oz [¾ cup] good dripping [beef fat]
pinch of cayenne pepper
salt and black pepper
mashed, well-seasoned potato for the last part of cooking

Put the fish into a greased oven-proof dish, add the dripping [beef fat], salt, black and cayenne pepper, and the chopped onion. Put on the lid and seal firmly.

Bake in moderate oven 190°C/375°F/ Gas Mark 5 until the fish is cooked through and tender. The time will depend upon the thickness of the pot; the thicker the pot the longer the cooking time.

When cooked, remove the fish from the pot, discard skin, bones, tails etc. Flake the fish and mix it into the seasoned mashed potato. Add the onion and any juices left in the fish pot and mix well again.

Put the well blended potato and fish mixture into another oven-proof dish and return to the oven without a lid to brown.

This dish can either be served straight from the oven in its pot, or the mixture can be formed into 'cakes', fairly large so they do not dry out, and served with parsley sauce.

PUNCH-NEP (A Welsh Turnip and Potato Tea or Supper Dish)

It was cold, bleak, biting weather: foggy withal: and he [Scrooge] could hear the people in the court outside, go wheezing up and down, beating their hands upon their breasts, and stamping their feet upon the pavement to warm them.

A Christmas Carol,
Charles Dickens, 1843

Scrooge and his poor clerk could have done with this warming dish of hot creamed potato and turnip. It is packed into a bowl and holes prodded into the top into which are poured melted buttered or warm cream, well seasoned.

Boil equal quantities of turnip and potato separately. When cooked, mash both with lots of cream, butter and black pepper and salt.

Blend the two vegetables together. Pack into a warm bowl, make small wells in the top and pour in the cream or butter.

Toast one side only of the bread. Spread the untoasted side with the cheese and bacon mixture. Grind a little black pepper over the top of each piece of toast and cheese. Grill gently until bubbling and golden. Serve at once.

NORTH COUNTRY CHEESE SAVOURY

A crimson smoulder in the West; The
    last late crow had won to rest;
A breath of ice that gripped the chest –
And freezing died the day
Melton and Homespun,
J. M. M. B. Durham ('Marshman') &
R. J. Richardson, 1913

This is an excellent recipe for using up any good flavoured crumbly cheese, as well as being quick to make when a cold, hungry hunter comes in for tea or supper.

To serve 4

1 small onion, peeled and finely chopped
¼ kg/8 oz [2 cups] cheese, such as
    Wensleydale, finely crumbled
4 rashers [slices] streaky bacon, rind
    removed
4 slices wholemeal [whole wheat] bread,
    home-made if possible
ground black pepper

Chop the bacon into small pieces. Put the onion and bacon into a pan and sauté together until the bacon and onion are just turning brown. Remove from the pan and mix with the crumbled cheese to make a thick paste.

EGG NOG

The squire always breakfasted on hunting mornings at 4 a.m. The meal consisted of underdone beef, washed down with eggs beaten up in brandy, and thus fortified, he was prepared for a fifty-mile ride if need be. It was no unusual thing to see Tom Moody, his famous whipper-in, taking the hounds to covert before daylight, and they would often stick to the sport till it was too dark to see the hounds.
'Squire' George Forester,
told by Thormanby, *c*1790

Take the yolks of two eggs and a tablespoon of sugar and beat to foam with a glass of brandy. Boil ½ litre/1 pint [2½ cups] of milk and pour over the egg mixture, stirring at low heat till a custard forms. Add shredded almonds and nutmeg and a very little finely cut candied lemon peel [zest]. Allow to cool. Next day beat the whites of the eggs with castor [superfine] sugar and brandy (only a flavouring), mix with an almost equal quantity of stiffly whipped and flavoured cream, and pile upon the custard just before serving.
Food in England,
Dorothy Hartley, 1954

BLACKBERRY AND ELDER WINE

The elderberry wine was reserved for winter evenings. About Christmas time, when the hours of darkness were long, and the whole family gathered about the blazing logs, the elder wine was brought out, mulled with spices and handed round as an innocent accompaniment to work and chat.

A Country Calendar, Flora Thompson

Combining the blackberries and elderberries together produces a rich, almost port-like wine. It is excellent for hip-flasks when out in the country on a cold winter's day, or sharing with friends by the fireside whatever the occasion.

To make 3½–4 litres/7–8 pints [8¾–10 US pints] wine

4 litres/8 pints [10 pints] water
¾ kg/1½ lb elderberries
¾ kg/1½ lb blackberries
juice and grated rind [zest] of 2 lemons
1½ kg/3 lb [6 cups] granulated sugar
15 g/½ oz wine or baker's yeast
1 stick cinnamon

Put the lemon peel [zest] and cinnamon into a muslin bag, leave a piece of thread to hang over the pan.

Into a large pan put the water and sugar. Immerse the spiced muslin bag into the water, hanging the thread over the side of the pan. Heat gently to dissolve the sugar, then simmer for 30 minutes. Remove the spiced muslin bag and any scum which may have formed on top of the liquid.

Wash the berries and drain well. Put them into a large bowl and mash them with a wooden spoon. Pour over the sugar syrup and mix well. Add the lemon juice, then allow to cool to 21°C/70°F.

Sprinkle the yeast over the liquid. Cover with a cloth, secure with string or elastic to prevent the cloth from sagging into the wine. Leave for 3 days, stirring about 3 times a day.

Strain the liquid into a 4 litre/8 pint [10 pint] fermenting jar, fill to the bottom of the neck. Fit an air-lock and leave until the fermentation has ceased. Rack as necessary, bottle and store.

Allow the wine to mature for at least 6 months before drinking, longer if it is possible to wait.

A SPORTSMAN'S PUNCH

An inch of snow fell last night and as we walked to Draycot to skate the snow storm began again. As we passed Langley Burrell Church we heard the strains of the quadrille band on the ice at Draycot . . . The Lancers was beautifully skated. When it grew dark the ice was lighted with Chinese lanterns, and the intense glare of blue, green, and crimson lights and magnesium riband made the whole place as light as day. Then people skated with torches.

Kilvert's Diaries, 1870

On such sporting or festive occasions, this heart-warming punch would go down very well. Serve it hot in small glasses and top them up often.

To make 25–30 glasses

3 bottles good Burgundy or Claret
8 whole cloves
2 oranges
8 tbsp brown raw cane sugar
1½ litres/3 pints [7½ cups] boiling water
225 ml/8 fl oz [1 cup] Cointreau or Grand
    Marnier
225 ml/8 fl oz [1 cup] brandy
225 ml/8 fl oz [1 cup] ginger wine

Pour the wine into a 5 litre/10 pint
preserving pan or saucepan (alternatively,
divide the recipe between two smaller
saucepans), add the sugar, cloves and
boiling water. Slice the oranges and add to
the pan. Cover and simmer for 30 minutes.

Remove from the heat and pour in the
ginger wine, brandy and Cointreau or
Grand Marnier. Give a few swirls round
with a ladle and serve in the warmed
glasses.

HOT SPICED TOMATO CUP

When we came within a town, and found
the church clocks all stopped, the dial-
faces choked with snow, and the inn-signs
blotted out, it seemed as if the whole place
were overgrown with white moss. As to
the coach, it was a mere snowball;– One
would have thought this enough : notwithstanding which, I pledge my word
that it snowed and snowed, and it still
snowed, and it never left off snowing.
                         Stopped by the Snow,
                 from *Christmas Stories,*
                 Charles Dickens, 1889

No doubt our traveller would have
welcomed a flask of this warming drink as
he travelled waist high in straw to keep
out the raw, winter weather. It can be
given extra spice by adding a glass of
sherry, but a little less stock is required if
sherry is added.

To make 6 cups

1 tsp curry paste
a few drops of tabasco sauce to taste
1 leaf each of rosemary, tarragon and basil
1 onion, peeled and sliced
400 ml/¾ pint [2 cups] chicken stock
540 ml/19 fl oz can tomato juice
glass of dry or medium sherry, optional

Pour the tomato juice over the sliced
onion. Put in the herbs. Allow to infuse in
the refrigerator for at least 2 hours.

Heat the chicken stock, mix in the
curry paste and tabasco sauce. Pour in the
tomato juice and herbs (and sherry, if
used), heat for a couple of minutes.

Strain the liquid into a flask or into
warmed cups. Discard the herbs and
onion.

A dab of whipped cream can be served
on top of the drink, sprinkled with black
pepper or cayenne pepper.

HOT TREACLE PUDDING

The snow in some places was almost up to the horses' shoulders. Towards Lynn the snow is much deeper and the road to it almost impassable. Will went on horseback with us to Norwich. We all dined, spent the Aft: supped &c. at the Kings Head.

The Diary of a Country Parson,
John Woodforde, 7 February 1784

The popularity of sweet and savoury pies and puddings has never diminished in Britain's long history of cooking. It is to be hoped that, with the weather as described above, Parson Woodforde and company found just such a pudding on the inn's menu, as this is one of the best for warming and filling the inner man after a day's sport or out in the frosty and snowy weather.

To serve approximately 6

60 g/2 oz [scant ¼ cup] black treacle
    [molasses] or golden [corn] syrup
¼ kg/8 oz [2 cups] self-raising flour [cake
    flour plus 1½ tsp baking powder]
1 egg, beaten
90 g/3 oz [scant ½ cup] shredded suet
60 g/2 oz [¼ cup] soft brown sugar
¼ tsp salt
2 tsps ground ginger
1 level tsp bicarbonate of soda
70 ml/2½ fl oz [¼ cup] milk

Mix the suet, brown sugar, ginger, flour, bicarbonate of soda and salt in a large bowl. Add the beaten egg, milk, treacle or syrup, stir well to a soft consistency. Pour into a greased 1 litre/2 pint pudding basin,

allowing 5 cm/2 in. spare at the top for the pudding to rise.

Cover the basin with greaseproof paper and secure with string. Stand the basin in a steamer or over a pan of boiling water, steam for 2 hours over a low heat. Top up the water from time to time as it evaporates.

When ready, turn onto a warm plate and serve with plenty of cream, with a little whisky added if desired, or extra treacle [molasses].

COUNTRY TREACLE TART

Coming home once from Eton for the Christmas holidays in bitterly cold weather with snow on the ground, I was so perished with cold that, instead of going into the Pelican at Newbury, and falling to on the excellent boiled or roast beef or mutton provided for the coach dinner, I ran to the saddler's and invested twelve shillings in a large and thick horse-rug, and was much laughed at for my pains, not only by my fellow passengers, but by my own family when I got home. However that evening coming over the Marlborough Downs between that town and Calne I think I had the laugh on my side.

Driving,
His Grace The Duke of Beaufort, KG, 1889

I should think that a piece of hot treacle tart would not be a bad investment either after travelling for miles on a bitter, cold winter's day.

During the eighteenth century in Scotland and the North, treacle or molasses was a favourite sweetener and was used for puddings and tarts well into the late eighteen hundreds, when a more refined, diluted type became available, known as golden syrup.

This pudding is a great favourite with John Oaksey, and after a day's racing commentary, on Britain's wintery and wind blown race courses, coming home to this sweet would be a very heart-warming thought, providing one isn't watching one's weight of course.

To serve 4–6 depending on appetites

180 g/6 oz shortcrust [pie] pastry
6 tbsp golden [corn] syrup
juice and grated rind [zest] of half a lemon
60 g/2 oz [scant ½ cup] fine, white breadcrumbs

Pre-heat the oven to 190°C/375°F/Gas Mark 5

Roll out the pastry and line a flan dish about 15 cm/6 in. to 20 cm/8 in. diameter with the rolled pastry.

Warm the syrup in a pan and stir in the lemon juice and rind [zest]. Sprinkle the breadcrumbs over the pastry case and pour in the warmed syrup. Cook for 30 to 35 minutes.

The tart can be eaten hot or cold, but if eaten hot, allow to cool a little or the bubbling syrup could burn the mouth. Serve with fresh pouring cream or if desired, cream to which a little brandy or whisky has been mixed in.

OLD FASHIONED PLUM PUDDING

Originally a meat stew to which the Elizabethans added prunes and herbs. Plum Pudding became associated with Christmas around the middle of the sixteenth century under the names Christmas porridge, broth or pottage. As fruit became more plentiful, currants, prunes and sultanas [golden raisins] were added and the meat phased out, as were for some reason the plums, although the fruit is still retained in its title.

After the first steaming, store in a well-ventilated, dry place for at least two to three months, longer if possible.

To make 3 puddings

500 g/1 lb [2 cups] soft dark brown sugar
1½ kg/2½ lb mixed fruit
250 g/½ lb dried apricots, chopped
125 g/¼ lb Brazil nuts, chopped
125 g/4 oz carrot, grated
500 g/1 lb apples, grated
350 g/¾ lb [2 cups] brown, wholemeal
    breadcrumbs
4 large eggs
2 tbsp malt or black treacle [molasses]
grated rind [zest] and juice of 2 oranges
grated rind [zest] and juice of 1 lemon
500 g/1 lb chopped suet
150 ml/¼ pint [½ cup] milk
wine glass dark rum or brandy
1 tsp salt

Put all the dry ingredients, including the fruit, apple and carrot into a large container.

Beat the egg, malt or treacle, milk, orange and lemon juice, grated rinds [zest] of the orange and lemon, rum or brandy together in a separate bowl.

Pour the liquid into the centre of the dry ingredients. Mix thoroughly together, cover, and leave overnight. (When mixing, do not forget to make a wish.)

Grease the insides of three 500 g/1 lb pudding basins and place a small round of greaseproof [wax] paper on the bottom of each basin. Fill with the pudding mixture, then cover the top with a further round of greaseproof [wax] paper, then a round of double thickness foil. Secure the edges around the basin.

Steam for 8 hours to produce a nice, dark pudding.

On the day required, steam for 3 hours. Turn the pudding out onto a warm serving dish, decorate with a sprig of holly, pour over a little previously heated brandy or rum and set alight, take to table flaming.

Serve with rum custard, brandy butter or double [heavy] cream.

APPLE BRANDY FLUMMERY

Refreshments – tea, coffee, ices, lemonade, and negus, handed round on trays, or set out in the ante-room, would be amply sufficient.

The Hunt Ball from
Handley Cross, R. S. Surtees, 1843

This is quite an unusual sweet, but one which is excellent for buffets or parties where food is left on the sideboard or table for guests to help themselves. It is served well chilled with a sweet oatmeal biscuit or shortbread fingers.

¼ litre/½ pint [1 cup] water
¾ kg/1½ lb eating apples, peeled, cored and
    sliced
60 g/2 oz [¼ cup] caster [superfine] sugar
    (a little more if you have a sweet tooth)
juice of 1 lemon
¼ litre/½ pint [1 cup] double [heavy] cream
2 sherry glasses brandy

Put the prepared apples into a saucepan with the water and bring to the boil. When the apple is soft, lower the heat and stir in the lemon juice, sugar and brandy.

When the sugar has dissolved, remove from the heat, allow to cool a little then liquidise and pour into a bowl.

Whip the cream lightly, then fold into the apple brandy mixture.

Put into a serving bowl or individual glass bowls and chill. Decorate when required, with slices of lemon and fresh apple pieces.

VICTORIAN WINTER PUDDING

During the Victorian era there were many hunting parsons. One such vicar was the Reverend J. P. Seasbrooke, who used to hunt with the Belvoir. Lady Augusta Fane tells us in her book *Chit-Chat*, that the Reverend's parishioners were so devoted to him, that they would never willingly disturb his pleasure by dying or getting married on hunting days. After a day's hunting, what better way to complete a dinner with this very delicious winter pudding. Rich and dark, ideal to satisfy even the most hungry of hunters.

125 g/4 oz [good ½ cup] demerara [light
    brown] sugar
3 fresh pears, peeled, cored and cut in half
    lengthways
6 halves of walnuts
125 g/4 oz Trex or Cookeen [shortening]
125 g/4 oz [¼ cup] golden [corn] syrup
125 g/4 oz [¼ cup] black treacle [molasses]
150 ml/¼ pint [½ cup] warm milk
2 small eggs
1 tsp bicarbonate of soda
125 g/4 oz [1 cup] unbleached plain [all
    purpose] white flour
125 g/4 oz [1 cup] wholemeal [whole
    wheat] flour
3 tsp ground ginger
2 tsp ground cinnamon
90 g/3 oz [½ cup] soft dark brown sugar
a little melted fat for the tin

Line the base of a 20 cm/8 in. round cake tin with greaseproof [wax] paper and brush over with melted fat. Sprinkle the base with the demerara sugar.

In the cavity of each pear half, press one walnut half. Place the pears, cut side down, into the base of the cake tin, on top of the demerara sugar, forming a circle around the edge of the tin.

Put the cooking fat into a pan and pour in the syrup and treacle. Heat gently until the fat has melted, put to one side.

Whisk the eggs and bicarbonate of soda together, then whisk in the milk.

Sift the two flours, the ginger and cinnamon into a large bowl, stir in the soft brown sugar.

Make a well in the centre and pour in the fat and syrup mixture and the egg and milk mixture; beat together for around 4 minutes until it is a smooth consistency.

Pour the cake mixture into the tin over the pear halves and bake for 45–50 minutes at 175°C/350°F/Gas Mark 4.

When cooked, turn out of the tin and serve with clotted or pouring cream.

HOT RUM BANANAS

The Exeter Fly has taken nearly three hours to come the seven miles from Hounslow. The landlord of The Bush, Staines, hearing this, follows the lead of the landlord of The George, and counsels rest and dinner; and the passengers, who to speak truly, have never before in their lives come so near to the experience of riding in the air in a hollowed-out iceberg, incline their ears to the advice.

Coaching Days and Coaching Ways,
W. Outram Tristram, 1893

After that fearful and freezing experience in the driving snow and howling wind, what a marvellous sight the inn lights would have been to the weary travellers and valiant coachman. This rum pudding, piping hot, would have warmed the hearts as well as the bodies of these intrepid travellers. It is a wonderful satisfying sweet for any traveller or visitor returning home to a blazing log fire and hot supper.

To serve 4

4 large or 8 small firm but ripe bananas
90 g/3 oz [6 tbsp] unsalted butter
6 tsp soft brown sugar
juice of 1 lemon
100 ml/4 fl oz [½ cup] dark rum

Melt the butter in a large heavy-based frying pan. Peel the bananas and cut them in half lengthways. Put the banana halves into the pan and shake over the sugar. Stir in the sugar and cook until the butter and sugar begin to caramelize. Turn the bananas carefully.

When the liquid has caramelized to a nutty brown colour, pour in the rum and lemon juice. Remove the bananas and put onto a hot serving dish. Boil the sauce rapidly for about one minute and pour over the bananas.

Serve with single, double [heavy] or clotted cream poured over. Greek yoghurt is also very good and contrasts and blends very well with the richness of the sauce.

ROLY-POLY JAM PUDDING

Roly-Poly – a childhood memory of schools and nurseries. It is also a delicious and satisfying pudding, especially when made with home-made jam. It can be baked or boiled but I think most people prefer it baked as the suety pudding and jam seem to have a richer flavour cooked in that way.

To serve 4–6

¼ kg/8 oz any home-made jam
180 g/6 oz suet crust pastry

Pre-heat the oven to 220°C/425°F/Gas Mark 7

Roll out the prepared pastry to a rectangle of about 18 cm/12 in. by 12 cm/8 in.

Thickly spread the pastry with the jam leaving a 1.5 cm/1 in. border of plain pastry around the edge.

Dampen the edges and roll up from the shortest side. Pinch the ends together to seal. Put the pudding onto a greased baking tray with the join underneath.

Bake for 40 minutes until it is a golden brown colour. If the pudding should brown too quickly, reduce the temperature to 200°C/400°F/Gas Mark 6.

When cooked, place onto a warm serving dish and serve with a home-made custard and/or more jam poured over. Double [heavy] cream will also go well if you do not want to make custard.

HOT COFFEE FUDGE PUDDING

'It's putrid weather,' agreed Lady Lomondham, pouring herself another cup from the Georgian coffee-pot. 'Still, I think I'd better make a one-horse day of it.'

Mustard-Pot, Huntsman,
Gilbert Frankau,
from The Horse Lover's Anthology, 1949

A delicious pudding for dessert or high tea. It separates during cooking thereby producing its own sauce, though it can be served with chilled sour cream, single [light] cream flavoured with coffee essence or with a fudge sauce if appetites are up to it.

To serve 8

6 tbsp coffee essence
360 g/12 oz [1½ cups] soft brown sugar
60 g/2 oz [½ cup] walnuts, chopped
250 g/8 oz [1 cup] butter
2 eggs, beaten
250 g/8 oz [2 cups] self-raising flour, sifted
      [cake flour plus 1½ tsp baking powder]
½ litre/1 pint [2½ cups] milk

Beat the butter and 250 g/8 oz [1 cup] sugar. Beat in the eggs gradually, then pour in the coffee essence. Gently fold in the flour and walnuts.

Add a little of the milk to give a dropping consistency. Spoon into a 2 litre/4 pint buttered oven-proof dish. Mix together the remaining milk and sugar and pour over the pudding.

Bake in the oven for 1 hour and 25 minutes, until it is spongy to the touch, 170°C/325°F/Gas Mark 3.

Serve as soon as it is cooked.

BRANDY SAUCE

It was during the seventeenth century that brandy was first introduced to England. Fishing ports became the haunts of smugglers seeing brandy as a prime cargo for profit. The government saw brandy as a profitable source of revenue and imposed a heavy customs duty upon it. Despite all these considerations, brandy was still easier to obtain and cheaper than tea or coffee. Time has made it easier for us all to obtain drink such as whisky or brandy, though in not so romantic or adventurous a fashion.

This brandy sauce is very good for accompanying a whole variety of sweets: any fruit, steamed or sponge pudding, pancakes, suet puddings, and of course the Christmas Pudding. Whisky can be substituted for brandy if desired.

To make 4–6 servings

4 tbsp brandy or whisky
2 tsp cornflour [cornstarch]
2 egg yolks, beaten
$\frac{1}{4}$ litre/$\frac{1}{2}$ pint [1$\frac{1}{4}$ cups] milk
2 tsp caster [superfine] sugar

Mix the cornflour [cornstarch] with two tbsp of the milk and mix to a paste. Heat the remaining milk in a pan until it just reaches boiling point. Remove from the heat and stir in the cornflour [cornstarch] paste.

Bring to the boil and cook for 5 minutes, stir constantly. Add the sugar, stir well and allow the sauce to cool for about 5 minutes.

Stir in the beaten egg yolks and then pour in the brandy or whisky. Place the pan over another saucepan of boiling water and cook until the sauce thickens. Stir constantly. The sauce must not boil at this stage; if it does, it will curdle.

Pour into a warm jug or over the desired pudding.

OLD ENGLISH RICH CHRISTMAS CAKE

To serve 8–10

1$\frac{1}{2}$ kg/3 lb mixed fruit
300 g/10 oz [2$\frac{1}{2}$ cups] plain [all purpose] flour
1 level tsp mixed spice
1 level tsp ground cinnamon
300 g/10 oz [1$\frac{1}{4}$ cups] butter
grated rind [zest] and juice of 1 lemon
300 g/10 oz [1$\frac{1}{4}$ cups] soft dark brown sugar
6 eggs, beaten
3 tbsp dark rum
125 g/4 oz split almonds
2 tbsp black treacle [molasses]

Line a 23 cm/9 in. cake tin with a double layer of greaseproof [wax] paper. Tie a double band of brown paper around the outside.

Put the flour into a bowl and add the spices. If necessary, clean the fruit then add to the flour and spices.

Cream the butter, sugar, lemon juice and peel [zest] together until pale and fluffy. Add the beaten eggs a little at a time, beating well after each addition. Pour in the black treacle [molasses] and beat again.

Fold in half the quantity of flour and fruit, mix well, then fold in the remaining half. Put in the almonds and pour in the rum. Mix well again, then put the mixture into a cake tin, spreading the mixture evenly.

Make a dip in the centre of the mixture to prevent the cake from rising during cooking. Stand the tin on a layer of brown paper in the bottom of the oven and bake for 4½ hours at 150°C/300°F/Gas Mark 1–2.

To avoid over browning, after 2½ hours cover the top of the cake with a couple of layers of greaseproof [wax] paper. When the cake is cooked, remove from the oven and allow to cool in the tin, then turn out onto a wire rack.

Before storing, the top of the cake can be pricked over with a fork, and an extra two or three tablespoons of brandy or dark rum can be added.

To store, wrap the cake in several layers of greaseproof [wax] paper and put into an air-tight tin. If a tin is not available, wrap round tightly with cooking foil.

FAT RASCALS

These cakes were once served in the inns of the Yorkshire Moors. They were cooked over a hot griddle, or in earlier days over a turf fire, where they went by the simpler name of Turf Cakes. The term 'rascal' is local dialect meaning 'a lean animal', and the 'fat' refers to the lard used in cooking. The name is a local contradiction in terms, epitomizing the Yorkshire sense of humour.

To make 24 cakes

1 egg, beaten with a little milk
250 g/8 oz [2 cups] self-raising flour [cake flour plus 1½ tsp baking powder]
125 g/4 oz [½ cup] lard
90 g/3 oz [scant ½ cup] sugar
¼ tsp salt
60 g/2 oz [scant ½ cup] currants
30 g/1 oz [¼ cup] sultanas [golden raisins]

Pre-heat the oven to 400°C/200°F/Gas Mark 6

Sieve the flour and the salt together. With the finger tips, rub in the lard until the mixture resembles breadcrumbs.

Stir in the currants, sugar and sultanas [golden raisins]. Add the beaten egg and mix well to a soft dough.

Roll out to a thickness of about 1.5 cm/½ in. and cut into rounds of about 5 cm/2 in. diameter.

Place them onto a greased baking tray and bake in the pre-heated oven for 15 minutes. The tray may need turning after about 7 minutes to prevent the cakes from burning.

SCOTTISH GINGER CAKE

Cauld blaws the wind frae east to west,
The drift is driving sairly,
Sae loud and shill's I hear the blast–
I'm sure it's winter fairly.

Cauld Blaws the Wind,
Robert Burns

On a cold winter's evening, what better thing to do than to have tea by a roaring fire when outside the wind blows and the snow is falling. Almost everyone would appreciate a piece of this homely cake accompanied by hot tea or a glass of ginger wine.

To serve 6–8

350 g/12 oz [3 cups] wholemeal [whole wheat] flour
½ tsp salt
2 level tsp bicarbonate of soda
4 tsp ground ginger
90 g/3 oz [½ cup] sultanas [golden raisins]
60 g/2 oz [scant ½ cup] preserved lemon and orange peel [zest], chopped
60 g/2 oz [scant ½ cup] chopped almonds
3 pieces preserved ginger, chopped
350 g/12 oz [1 cup] black treacle [molasses]
180 g/6 oz [¾ cup] butter
90 g/3 oz [½ cup] soft brown sugar
3 eggs, beaten
2 tbsp milk

Pre-heat the oven to 160°C/325°F/Gas Mark 3

Grease and line a 18 cm/7 in. square cake tin with silicone paper.

Sift the flour, salt, ground ginger and bicarbonate of soda into a bowl.

Put the treacle [molasses], butter and sugar into a saucepan and heat gently, do not boil.

To the flour mixture, add the preserved lemon and orange peel, sultanas, almonds and preserved ginger pieces. Mix thoroughly then make a well in the centre and pour in the milk and beaten egg. Beat well, then pour in the treacle and sugar mixture and beat all together until well blended. (This process can be done in a blender but do not add the almonds or sultanas until well creamed or they will break up too much.)

Pour the mixture into the prepared cake tin and cook for 2 to 2½ hours.

This cake keeps very well for about a week.

WHIG OR WIG CAKES

There are various stories surrounding the origins of wig cakes, from a seventeenth century breakfast accompaniment, to being served with punch or mulled wine on Christmas Eve in Victorian times. The name wig came from the wedge-shaped wheat dough made by the baker. Whatever their origin, these spicy dough cakes are delicious and will accompany your breakfast marmalade or hot drinks on a cold winter's night.

To make 16 wigs or wedges

1 pkt Harvest Gold yeast or 15 g/½ oz
    fresh yeast or 2 level tsp dried yeast
225 ml/8 fl oz [1 cup] warm milk
500 g/1 lb [4 cups] plain [all purpose]
    flour
150 g/5 oz [10 tbsp] unsalted butter,
    softened
½ tsp ground ginger
½ tsp ground mixed spice
2 tsp caraway seeds (optional)
125 g/4 oz [good ½ cup] caster [superfine]
    sugar

If using fresh yeast, cream with the warm milk before adding to the dry ingredients.

Mix the dry yeast or Harvest Gold with the dry ingredients then gradually pour in the warm milk. Add the softened butter and knead together until a soft dough is formed. Cover with a polythene [polyethylene] and put in a warm place to prove for around two hours.

Grease two 20 cm/8 in. tins and when the dough has proved, divide into two equal pieces. A little extra flour may be necessary if the dough is sticky to handle. Press each piece of dough into the greased tins, cut across four times to produce eight wedges to each piece. Prove again for 20 minutes.

Bake for 15 to 20 minutes at 200°C/400°F/Gas Mark 5. Eat hot straight from the oven.

INDEX

153